6-10-89

To Suzanne + ...
The very best of wishes
To a special couple.
From
Calvin + Rozella
Broadhead

The POWER
AND THE
PROMISE

The POWER
AND THE
PROMISE

S. Michael Wilcox

Bookcraft
Salt Lake City, Utah

Library of Congress Catalog Card Number: 89-60570

ISBN 0-88494-696-7

First Printing, 1989

Printed in the United States of America

To those "fathers" who honored and bequeathed the sacred trust of the priesthood, enabling me and my posterity to share in God's work through the authority we humbly attempt to bear.

Now the great and grand secret of the whole matter, and the *summum bonum* of the whole subject that is lying before us, consists in obtaining the powers of the Holy Priesthood. For him to whom these keys are given there is no difficulty in obtaining a knowledge of facts in relation to the salvation of the children of men, both as well for the dead as for the living

—D&C 128:11

Contents

Preface

I approach this topic of the Melchizedek Priesthood with great humility. I have ever felt that the privilege of holding the Melchizedek Priesthood was one of the greatest gifts God bestows upon his sons. Its blessings to women and to all of mankind are a strong evidence of a loving Father in Heaven. What a tremendous trust we hold!

I have not attempted to write an exhaustive commentary on the Melchizedek Priesthood. There are many important areas connected with the priesthood, such as ordinances, that I have not touched upon. This is not because I consider them unimportant but rather because I felt this information was better dealt with in other manuals, articles, and books. I have, however, tried to capture the essence of the priesthood by examining the principles upon which it rests and upon which its powers can be released. In short, because Melchizedek means king of righteousness, I have tried to define what a true king of righteousness is and does. In so doing, I have written of attitudes, intelligence, prophets, families, and priestcraft; of winning hearts, teaching the sons of Aaron, and fulfilling the Abrahamic covenant with its sacred responsibilities. I have also tried to give a fuller meaning to the words "magnify your calling, honor your priesthood."

I have tried to draw the truths of the priesthood from the scriptures. Taken as a whole, the standard works paint a very detailed picture. When we see it in totality, the scope of the priesthood fills us with a humility born of realizing the depth of honor we have been given by sharing in God's work in such an intimate way. Perhaps no mortal writer can find words beautiful and powerful enough to fit the dignity of God's priesthood; only the scriptures can do that as they are read under the influence of the Holy Ghost. With this limitation in mind, let us seek clarification, understanding, and fulfillment in the scriptures.

To the sisters of the Church who read these pages I would like to say this: Although the focus of this book is directed to the brethren of the Church, its principles are important for women to understand as they share in the blessings of the priesthood through their fathers, husbands, sons, and leaders. Many of the principles discussed herein are empty without the support, understanding, love, and companionship of a wife and mother. The scriptural truths which govern the priesthood are applicable in most instances to the central role women play in our Father in Heaven's glorious plan of salvation. By emphasizing the role of the priesthood I by no means wish to deemphasize that of mothers and wives, for without them the priesthood loses its greatest significance.

But ye are a chosen generation, a royal
priesthood, an holy nation, a peculiar people;
that ye should shew forth the praises of him
who hath called you out of darkness into his
marvellous light.

— 1 Peter 2:9

CHAPTER ONE

Peace and Righteousness

I can remember each of my ordinations in the priesthood and
have always looked with awe and wonder upon holding God's
authority. The thought that an ordinary man such as I am, with
weaknesses and limitations, can be entrusted with the responsibilities of priesthood authority is often overwhelming.

The scriptures have much to say about the priesthood and
man's relationship to it. The focus for our study, then, will be
the scriptures, for we can have complete faith in the truths we
may glean from these inspired sources.

Seeking the Priesthood

The scriptures teach that men should possess certain attitudes before they receive the priesthood. These attitudes should
continue to grow and deepen throughout a man's life, thus play-
ing a major role in a man's ability to honor his priesthood and
magnify his callings in that priesthood. Abraham exemplified
these desirable attitudes even prior to receiving his ordination:

And, finding there was greater happiness and peace and rest for me, I sought for the blessings of the fathers, and the right whereunto I should be ordained to administer the same; having been myself a follower of righteousness, desiring also to be one who possessed great knowledge, and to be a greater follower of righteousness, and to possess a greater knowledge, and to be a father of many nations, a prince of peace, and desiring to receive instructions, and to keep the commandments of God, I became a rightful heir, a High Priest, holding the right belonging to the fathers (Abraham 1:2).

Much truth is taught about the priesthood in this single verse. Notice Abraham's desire to receive the priesthood. This was not a mild desire, but an active pursuit and preparation. In verse 4 Abraham tells us, "I sought for mine appointment unto the Priesthood." The priesthood ought to be greatly desired and sought for. This attitude implies that the bearer of the priesthood knows its value and properly views it as something more than advancement that comes automatically with increasing age.

Happiness, Peace, and Rest

Abraham desired and sought the priesthood for specific reasons. He was not looking for personal aggrandizement or honor; he sought his appointment because he knew he could obtain greater happiness, peace, and rest through the blessings the priesthood bestows. That is not his only reason for seeking the priesthood, however. Abraham also desired "the right . . . to administer the same." Apparently his attention was turned outward to those who would receive his ministrations, and certainly his later life suggests that he desired happiness, peace, and rest for them. Desiring to bring happiness, peace, and rest to God's other children should be a key attitude for a priesthood bearer. He must realize and have a testimony that "greater" happiness, peace, and rest come through the blessings of the priesthood, and must desire that all receive these blessings.

Follower of Righteousness

A person's ability to bless others is dependent on his or her own righteousness. Therefore, it was essential that Abraham desire to be a follower of righteousness. He tells us that he had qualified himself to hold the priesthood by being "a follower of righteousness." The prophet Alma speaks eloquently of such preparation. He details the characteristics one should manifest before receiving the priesthood.

> And this is the manner after which they were ordained — being called and prepared from the foundation of the world according to the foreknowledge of God, *on account of their exceeding faith and good works*; in the first place being left to choose good or evil; *therefore they having chosen good, and exercising exceedingly great faith*, are called with a holy calling, yea, with that holy calling which was prepared with, and according to, a preparatory redemption for such.
> And thus they have been called to this holy calling *on account of their faith*, while others would reject the Spirit of God on account of the hardness of their hearts and blindness of their minds, while, if it had not been for this they might have had as great privilege as their brethren. (Alma 13:3–4, italics added.)

Thus we see that faith, good works, and accepting the guidance of the Spirit should precede priesthood ordination. This is implied in the opening verse of the oath and covenant of the priesthood given in the Doctrine and Covenants: "For whoso is faithful unto the obtaining these two priesthoods of which I have spoken, and the magnifying their calling, are sanctified by the Spirit unto the renewing of their bodies" (D&C 84:33). God expects us to be faithful before receiving the priesthood.

Abraham, however, is not satisfied with his initial righteousness and faithfulness. He wants to be "a greater follower of righteousness." Christ required this attitude of his disciples when he told them to "hunger and thirst after righteousness" (Matthew 5:6). A priesthood bearer should have this thirst, and his

actions should manifest it. He should want righteousness so
deeply that he needs it as his body needs water and bread. The
greater his degree of personal integrity, righteousness, and character, the better he will be able to administer the blessings of the
gospel. His ability to "administer" happiness, peace, and rest
will be magnified by his becoming "a greater follower of righteousness."

Greater Knowledge

If we follow a path leading to greater righteousness, we will
find ourselves possessing greater knowledge. This is a natural
law of God's kingdom. Light, truth, and intelligence are given to
individuals as their righteousness increases. Alma taught that
"he that will harden his heart, the same receiveth the lesser portion of the word; and he that will not harden his heart, to him is
given the greater portion of the word, until it is given unto him to
know the mysteries of God until he know them in full" (Alma
12:10).

This same truth is detailed many times in the Doctrine and
Covenants. A few examples will strengthen our understanding:
"He that keepeth his commandments receiveth truth and light,
until he is glorified in truth and knoweth all things" (D&C
93:28). Keeping the commandments produces for the obedient
greater light and truth. "That which is of God is light," section
50 of the Doctrine and Covenants teaches, "and he that receiveth light, and continueth in God, receiveth more light; and
that light groweth brighter and brighter until the perfect day"
(D&C 50:24).

Character, integrity, and a thirst for righteousness produce a
godly knowledge. It is evident from Abraham 1:2 that Abraham
desired great knowledge. He was willing to follow righteousness
in order to possess "greater knowledge," or to obtain understanding of the "mysteries of God" spoken of by Alma. This desire to progress in the knowledge of godliness is an important attitude of the righteous priesthood holder today.

There is a significant reason why a man should want greater
knowledge. It is not to build up himself in others' eyes as one
with superior understanding. This is the pride of worldly
knowledge. The greater knowledge that Abraham sought enables the priesthood bearer to bless and minister happiness,

peace, and rest to others. It is therefore essential that the bearer of this greater knowledge focus his labors on serving others, as Alma the Elder plainly taught the priests he ordained to minister over the Nephite church. These "priests were not to depend upon the people for their support; but for their labor they were to receive the grace of God, that they might wax strong in the Spirit, having the knowledge of God, that they might teach with power and authority from God" (Mosiah 18:26).

Receiving Instructions

Another attitude indicated in Abraham 1:2 warrants attention. Abraham explains that he desired "to receive instructions, and to keep the commandments of God," revealing an attitude of obedience and love toward the teachings, counsels, and commandments of God. Abraham wanted the commandments and teachings of the Father so that he could be a follower of righteousness and obtain greater knowledge. Not only did he want to receive these instructions and commandments, but he also intended to "keep" them.

Abraham exhibited four major attitudes that priesthood holders should cultivate when they prepare to receive the priesthood and develop as they seek to magnify their callings in it: (1) a desire to bring happiness, peace, and rest to oneself and others by administering the blessings of the priesthood; (2) a desire to be a better follower of righteousness through the constant molding of a Christlike character; (3) a desire to possess greater and greater knowledge, light, and truth concerning the mysteries of God and the doctrines and covenants of his gospel; (4) a desire to receive instruction, counsel, and commandments from God, as well as a commitment to keep the commandments. These four attitudes are so basic to the gospel that all who seek to become disciples of Christ need to cultivate them.

Prince of Peace

Possessing these attitudes and desires will cause a man to honor his priesthood and magnify his callings in it. These are key principles that help lead a man to become a "prince of peace." What is the significance of the title "prince of peace"? Where did Abraham get this title, and what does it have to do with the priesthood?

To understand the answers to these questions we need to know more about a contemporary of Abraham named Melchizedek. In Genesis 14 we read that "Melchizedek king of Salem . . . was the priest of the most high God. And he blessed him, and said, Blessed be Abram of the most high God, possessor of heaven and earth. . . . And he gave him tithes of all." (Genesis 14:18–20.) Abraham acknowledged Melchizedek's priesthood authority and paid tithes to him. This incident is referred to in both the Book of Mormon and the Joseph Smith Translation of the Bible. In these two additional accounts we learn much more about Melchizedek. Alma explained the following about him:

> Now this Melchizedek was a king over the land of Salem; and his people had waxed strong in iniquity and abomination; yea, they had all gone astray; they were full of all manner of wickedness;
> But Melchizedek having exercised mighty faith, and received the office of the high priesthood according to the holy order of God, did preach repentance unto his people. And behold, they did repent; and Melchizedek did establish peace in the land in his days; *therefore he was called the prince of peace,* for he was the king of Salem; and he did reign under his father. (Alma 13:17–18, italics added.)

Melchizedek, faced with the wickedness of his people and having received the priesthood, taught repentance and established peace. This is the peace that comes from righteousness and obedience. Thus, at the Last Supper Christ promised his followers that he would leave peace with them: "Peace I leave with you, my peace I give unto you: not as the world giveth, give I unto you" (John 14:27). Abraham desired this greater peace for himself and recognized that it came in part through righteous bearing of the priesthood (see Abraham 1:2). Because Melchizedek, through his priesthood, brought peace to his land, "he was called the prince of peace."

The Joseph Smith Translation of Genesis 14 brings out the same truths. Melchizedek was "approved of God" and "ordained an high priest" (JST, Genesis 14:27; see verses 25–40).

Obviously, through faith and good works he had prepared himself for his ordination. We read of Melchizedek's youth and some of the powers of the priesthood that he had already exercised, and then comes the following:

> And now, Melchizedek was a priest of this order; therefore *he obtained peace in Salem, and was called the Prince of peace.*
>
> And his people wrought righteousness, and obtained heaven, and sought for the city of Enoch which God had before taken, separating it from the earth, having reserved it unto the latter days, or the end of the world. . . .
>
> And this Melchizedek, having thus established righteousness, was called the *king of heaven* by his people, or, in other words, the *King of peace.* (JST, Genesis 14:33–34, 36, italics added.)

Once again the title "Prince of peace" is used, accompanied by the title "King of peace," and given to Melchizedek because he established righteousness among his people.

The responsibility to turn people from a state of wickedness to one of righteousness is at the very center of the priesthood, both Aaronic and Melchizedek. It is one of the most important challenges given to the Church. Speaking to the Levitical priests of Malachi's day concerning his original covenant with Levi, the Lord emphasizes this responsibility and speaks of other truths we have also seen in Abraham 1:2. "The law of truth was in his mouth, and iniquity was not found in his lips: he walked with me in peace and equity, and did turn many away from iniquity. For the priest's lips should keep knowledge, and they should seek the law at his mouth: for he is the messenger of the Lord of hosts." (Malachi 2:6–7.)

Let us now examine one more scriptural account of Melchizedek, this one found in Paul's epistle to the Hebrews:

> For this Melchisedec, king of Salem, priest of the most high God, who met Abraham returning from the slaughter of the kings, and blessed him;
>
> To whom also Abraham gave a tenth part of all; *first being by interpretation King of righteousness, and after that also King of Salem, which is, King of peace;*

For this Melchizedek was ordained a priest after the order of the Son of God, which order was without father, without mother, without descent, having neither beginning of days, nor end of life. *And all those who are ordained unto this priesthood are made like unto the Son of God,* abiding a priest continually. (JST, Hebrews 7:1-3, italics added.)

Paul tells us a number of things in this verse. The name *Melchizedek* is also a title, which literally means "King of righteousness" and is closely associated with "King of peace." The Joseph Smith Translation of these verses teaches priesthood bearers an important truth: "All those who are ordained unto this priesthood are made like unto the Son of God, abiding a priest continually." Recognizing this truth will help men who hold the Melchizedek Priesthood understand the power and the significance of what they bear. They will realize what an honor and privilege it is to hold this sacred trust.

We can now see the significance of Abraham's desire to be a "prince of peace." He was following the example of Melchizedek, who was following the prophesied example of Christ. It is apparent that the most worthy person to hold the title of Prince of Peace and King of Righteousness is Christ. Isaiah used this title when he described the Savior in prophetic vision: "For unto us a child is born, unto us a son is given: and the government shall be upon his shoulder: and his name shall be called Wonderful, Counsellor, The mighty God, The everlasting Father, *The Prince of Peace*" (Isaiah 9:6, italics added). This is the very essence of priesthood. Each man can become a prince of peace and a king of righteousness by following the example of the Savior.

When we are baptized we take upon ourselves the name of Christ. When we have the rebirth of the Spirit, he takes us into his family, and through his atonement we become his sons and daughters, bearing his name. Each time we partake of the sacrament we recovenant with God to take the Savior's name upon us, to remember him, and keep his commandments. When a man receives the priesthood, he takes another step. Christ has given his followers who hold the priesthood an opportunity to share some important titles—prince of peace and king of righteousness. Priesthood holders should do with their priesthood what Christ did with his, and what Melchizedek did with his. They should seek to establish peace and righteousness; they should lift their fellow beings to higher levels, just as Melchizedek helped his people to "[work] righteousness and obtain heaven" and as Christ lifted all mankind with his life, teachings, and Atonement.

These truths dovetail perfectly with Abraham's desire to administer happiness, peace, and rest. In very simple terms, this is what the oath and covenant suggests when it uses the term *magnify* in regard to the priesthood's various callings. A man magnifies and honors his calling when he establishes righteousness, peace, and rest, for that is what Christ did. In this manner a priesthood holder is "made like unto the Son of God" and becomes a prince of peace, a king of righteousness.

It might be helpful to examine a few additional scriptures that relate to Melchizedek. In Doctrine and Covenants 107 we learn of the reason for naming the priesthood Melchizedek. "Why the first is called the Melchizedek Priesthood is because Melchizedek was such a great high priest. Before his day it was called the *Holy Priesthood, after the Order of the Son of God.*" (D&C 107:2–3.) Melchizedek was so honored because he was "such a great high priest." In other words, he fulfilled the responsibilities of the priesthood so completely that his name and title could appropriately be forever linked to God's authority and power. All holders of this priesthood can become Melchizedeks or kings of righteousness in their own right by following the example laid down in the scriptures.

There are some indications that Melchizedek had another name and was called Melchizedek or king of righteousness only because of his use of the priesthood. In Doctrine and Covenants 138:41, Shem is referred to as "the great high priest." It is possible that Shem's righteousness earned him the title of Melchizedek and that the title eventually became synonymous with his name. However, the relationship of Shem to Melchizedek is not certain, and what is important is the activity and righteousness of the man we know as Melchizedek, regardless of whether he was known by any other name. He honored his priesthood so faithfully that he became what his name and title meant. What a wonderful example for all priesthood holders to follow!

Once we have this perspective on the priesthood, many
verses of scripture begin to take on more meaning. Isaiah gave a
beautiful description that can be applied to the mission of Melchizedek Priesthood bearers who desire to become true princes
of peace. "How beautiful upon the mountains are the feet of him
that bringeth good tidings," he wrote, "that publisheth peace;
that bringeth good tidings of good, that publisheth salvation;
that saith unto Zion, Thy God reigneth!" (Isaiah 52:7.)

Abinadi interpreted this verse and expanded it to include
those who had published the peace of Christ's gospel, past and
present, and those who would publish it in the future. All of the
prophets and righteous sharers of the gospel in all ages can be
included in this verse. Abinadi then centers its meaning on the
Prince of Peace himself by stating, "O how beautiful upon the
mountains are the feet of him that bringeth good tidings, that is
the founder of peace, yea, even the Lord, who has redeemed his
people; yea, him who has granted salvation unto his people"
(Mosiah 15:18).

Tying all these ideas together, we can see some added significance in the promise John gave followers of Christ when he
said: "Beloved, now are we the sons of God, and it doth not yet
appear what we shall be: but we know that, when he shall appear, we shall be like him; for we shall see him as he is" (1 John
3:2). For a holder of the Melchizedek Priesthood to be "like
him" entails the ability to function as an honorable king of righteousness and prince of peace. Earth life can be viewed as an apprenticeship for that exaltation in the eternities. Therefore, it is
absolutely critical that holders of the priesthood magnify their
callings (see D&C 84:33).

The highest and most beautiful promises relative to these
teachings are given in the temple. It would be well for all priesthood holders to ponder again the covenants and promises they
made and received in the temple. If they will fulfill those ordinances through living a faithful life, they will receive the throne
of Christ, as spoken of by John in several places in his Revelation. Thus he wrote, "To him that overcometh will I grant to sit
with me in my throne, even as I also overcame, and am set down
with my Father in his throne" (Revelation 3:21). Later he recorded that Christ, through his sacrifice, "hast made us unto our
God kings and priests: and we shall reign on the earth" (Revela-

tion 5:10). We have taken Christ's name in baptism; we share his title in the reception of the priesthood; may we live worthy of receiving his throne as he has promised the faithful.

Father of Many Nations

Let us now return to Abraham 1:2 and attempt to understand one last phrase. Abraham desired to be a "father of many nations." Does this phrase have as much significance as "prince of peace" when examined in the context of the priesthood Abraham desired to administer?

The promise given to Abraham of an abundant posterity was repeated on several occasions. In Haran, Abraham was promised, "I will make of thee a great nation" (Abraham 2:9). Later, in the land of Canaan, God repeated this promise, using the heavens to illustrate his point: "And he brought him forth abroad, and said, Look now toward heaven, and tell the stars, if thou be able to number them: and he said unto him, So shall thy seed be" (Genesis 15:5).

When Abraham was ninety-nine, before the birth of Isaac, the Lord once again assured him that he would be a father of many nations. At this time the Lord changed Abraham's name from Abram to Abraham, which means literally "father of a multitude" (see LDS Bible Dictionary, "Abraham"). "As for me, behold, my covenant is with thee, and thou shalt be a father of many nations. Neither shall thy name any more be called Abram, but thy name shall be Abraham; for a father of many nations have I made thee." (Genesis 17:4–5.) It is obvious from these references that the Lord promised Abraham that he would indeed become a father of many nations as he desired and that this promise constituted a major aspect of the Abrahamic covenant.

Even a cursory search of the historical record will reveal that Abraham's descendants did indeed produce a multitude of nations and people. Literally millions of earth's inhabitants share Abraham as their ancestor, through Isaac, Ishmael, or Keturah's sons. However, other aspects of this promise are inseparably connected with the priesthood. One of these promises is given in Abraham 2, which we will examine in greater detail later in this book. Another is explained in Doctrine and Covenants 132. An examination of both promises in the context of Abraham's becoming a father of many nations may offer deeper insight into attitudes associated with the priesthood.

Sons of Abraham

While Abraham was living in Haran, before his departure for the land of Canaan, the Lord promised him that "as many as receive this Gospel shall be called after thy name, and shall be accounted thy seed, and shall rise up and bless thee, as their father" (Abraham 2:10). Thus, all true followers of the gospel become the seed of Abraham, and in this way Abraham is the father of "many nations."

The Lord continues speaking with Abraham, giving us further light on the relationship of this promise to the priesthood: "In thee (that is, in thy Priesthood) and in thy seed (that is, thy Priesthood), for I give unto thee a promise that this right shall continue in thee, and in thy seed after thee (that is to say, the literal seed, or the seed of the body) shall all the families of the earth be blessed, even with the blessings of the Gospel, which are the blessings of salvation, even of life eternal" (Abraham 2:11). According to this revelation, all who hold the priesthood are called the sons or "seed" of Abraham. This blessing is significant for all priesthood holders. Much of that significance we will discuss later when we talk of the Abrahamic covenant as it relates more specifically to the priesthood. For the present it is important to see the dignity of becoming a son of Abraham through receiving the priesthood.

Many parents name their children after great men. I have a son named Benjamin, after King Benjamin, one named Adam, and one named McKay. I want my sons to grow up to be as noble and righteous as those for whom they were named. A true "son of Abraham" will seek the works, righteousness, and desires of his "father." He will try to live up to that name. Therefore, in order to magnify his calling in the priesthood, a priesthood holder must strive to work righteousness as Abraham did, to follow his example even as Abraham followed the example of Melchizedek, the great patriarchs, and the Savior.

The Promise of Eternal Lives

Those who work righteousness as Abraham did have the same promises of blessings as he had. The greatest of these blessings reach fulfillment in the eternities ahead and are set forth in section 132 of the Doctrine and Covenants. This revelation centers on the concept of eternal marriage, the highest ordinance open to mankind on the earth and the key to receiving eternal life. It promises the gift of exaltation or godhood to those who enter the covenant of eternal marriage and live righteous lives. Those who fulfill the covenant by enduring to the end are assured of "eternal life," or an eternal increase. The Lord promises that this "glory shall be a fulness and a continuation of the seeds forever and ever" (D&C 132:19). After detailing the particulars of this promise, the Lord speaks of the priesthood and then of the patriarch Abraham:

> Abraham received promises concerning his seed, and of the fruit of his loins—from whose loins ye are, namely, my servant Joseph—which were to continue so long as they were in the world; and as touching Abraham and his seed, *out of the world they should continue; both in the world and out of the world should they continue as innumerable as the stars;* or, if ye were to count the sand upon the seashore ye could not number them.
>
> *This promise is yours* also, because ye are of Abraham, and the promise was made unto Abraham. (D&C 132:30–31, italics added.)

From such passages we understand more completely the meaning of God's promise that Abraham would have a multitudinous posterity. The broader fulfillment of this will come about in the eternities, where Abraham as a god, possessing the power of eternal increase, will continue to be a father over posterity as innumerable as the stars. Thus he does the work of God, contributing to the continuation of the Father's "work and glory" (see Moses 1:39).

This promise to Abraham is extended to all who "are of Abraham," meaning to all Melchizedek Priesthood bearers (who are his seed) and to all God's children, male and female, who accept his gospel, live its principles, and enter and remain faithful to an eternal marriage relationship through the priesthood sealing power of the temple.

This eternal life and increase of his children is the very essence of the Father's glorification (see D&C 132:31). Thus through temple ordinances priesthood bearers and their eternal companions are invited to participate in the work and continued glorification of their Father in Heaven and his children. The Father's work is the happiness, peace, and rest of his children. He does this work throughout all eternity. Is it any wonder that a man's most important priesthood function centers in the home and family, just as a woman's most important calling is that of wife and mother? To fulfill their priesthood responsibility at its most sacred level, fathers must bring happiness, peace, rest, and the blessings of the gospel to their families, for those families will continue and increase forever. Fathers are meant to be kings of righteousness in the most important domain or kingdom to which they belong, that of their own families. This they cannot do without an eternal relationship formed in the holy temple.

With this in mind it is possible to discover scriptural truth regarding how a man truly becomes a prince of peace, a king of righteousness, in his home with the help of his wife.

In the celestial glory there are three heavens
or degrees; and in order to obtain the highest,
a man must enter into this order of the priesthood [meaning the new and everlasting covenant of marriage]; and if he does not, he cannot obtain it. He may enter into the other, but
that is the end of his kingdom; he cannot
have an increase.

—D&C 131:1–4

CHAPTER TWO

Priesthood in Marriage

This life can be seen as an apprenticeship for godhood. The Lord
has provided us with all the tools necessary to learn to do the
work of our Father in Heaven. What is that work? It is beautifully explained in simple, comprehensive terms in the book of
Moses: "For behold, this is my work and my glory—to bring to
pass the immortality and eternal life of man" (Moses 1:39). God
creates, has children, and then works to exalt them. Everything
he does enhances this work. Worlds are created, prophets are
called, scriptures are written, an atonement is made—all for the
purpose of exalting his children and blessing them with eternal
life.

God is a father. It is no coincidence that he has chosen this
term by which to be called. As priesthood holders, men should
seek to prove to God that they can be fathers in the truest sense,
just as women strive to be noble mothers. This is a major aspect
of their apprenticeship. God, therefore, eager to let his children
learn the great lesson of exaltation and desirous that the plan of
salvation go forth, grants them the ability to procreate. This gift
of procreation is sacred because it is godly. Men aspiring to eter-

nal life are required to prove to God that they will use the pro-creative gift righteously—that is, to bind themselves to their wives in oneness of love and to bring children into the world. To use this godlike power selfishly for gratification, lust, or any other unrighteous motive is to act contrary to the work of God. When men act in this way they dishonor the priesthood in one of its most sacred areas of responsibility—the family.

When our Father in Heaven sends children into a home, he expects the priesthood bearer and earthly father to lift, inspire, and help to exalt those children, for in so doing that father engages in the work of God. In this manner—if done consistently over time—a man can "prove" to God that he is worthy to be a "father of many nations" throughout the eternities. He of course shares this responsibility with his companion with whom he must establish unity and oneness. Thus, how a priesthood bearer deals with his dual responsibility as both husband and father is critical to exaltation.

To Be One

The Savior often taught the principle of oneness. "If ye are not one ye are not mine," he said (D&C 38:27). He used his own oneness with the Father as an example. A husband who is magnifying his priesthood callings will seek to establish oneness with his wife. God has stressed this oneness from the very beginning: "It was not good that the man should be alone; wherefore, I will make an help meet for him" (Moses 3:18).

Many people misread this scripture by combining in their minds the words *help* and *meet*. But in the scriptures the words are separated into noun and adjective. A wife is a "help" that is "meet" for her husband. What does *meet* mean? In Hebrew the prime root means literally to surround, protect, or aid, in English the word means suitable, proper, and so on. Thus, as used in this scripture the word carries a connotation that suggests an equality between woman and man. A marriage in which the wife serves as a "help" will promote a oneness in a marriage relationship. Man is not an overlord, but rather needs a help "meet" for him.

In this connection we can see in the story of the rib, the figurative account of the creation of Eve, a powerful metaphor about marriage. President Harold B. Lee explained this as follows:

> In defining the relationship of a wife to her husband, the late President George Albert Smith put it this way: "In showing this relationship, by a symbolic representation, God didn't say that woman was to be taken from a bone in the man's head that she should rule over him, nor from a bone in his foot that she should be trampled under his feet, but from a bone in his side to symbolize that she was to stand by his side, to be his companion, his equal, and his helpmeet in all their lives together." (*Ye Are the Light of the World* [Salt Lake City: Deseret Book Co., 1974], p. 284.)

Wishing to stress the importance of oneness in a marriage, God taught Adam to understand that Eve was now "bone of my bones, and flesh of my flesh" (Moses 3:23). To further enhance the depth of this relationship, the scriptures say, "Therefore shall a man leave his father and his mother, and shall cleave unto his wife; and they shall be one flesh" (Moses 3:24). We see significance in the statement that the man leaves his father and mother to cleave to his wife (rather than the wife leaving her parents to cleave to her husband) when we realize the strong, filial bonds of the father-son relationships in the ancient world. The Lord wanted no question about the responsibility of the husband to cleave to his wife above all other people. Thus, a priesthood holder will see that a proper relationship with his wife will express a true "oneness."

Maintaining a Oneness

The oneness of a husband and wife can be maintained only in the Lord's way. The scriptures teach that method in many places. I will refer to only two. The first is the counsel of the Apostle Paul, the second that of the Prophet Joseph Smith.

Paul compares the love of a husband for his wife to the love of Christ for the Church. God has often used the metaphor of a bridegroom and his bride to explain the relationship of the Savior to the Church. Christ is the King of Righteousness, the Prince of Peace. How does he treat his bride, the Church? In his example all who would be kings of righteousness will find understanding for treating their own brides. Paul teaches:

> Husbands, *love your wives,* even as Christ also loved the church, and *gave himself* for it;
> That he might sanctify and cleanse it with the washing of water by the word,
> That he might present it to himself a glorious church, not having spot, or wrinkle, or any such thing; but that it should be *holy and without blemish.*
> So ought men to love their wives as their own bodies. He that loveth his wife loveth himself.
> For no man ever yet hated his own flesh; but *nourisheth* and *cherisheth* it, even as the Lord the church. . . .
> For this cause shall a man leave his father and mother, and shall be joined unto his wife, and *they two shall be one flesh.* (Ephesians 5:25–29, 31, italics added.)

Paul tells us how a couple becomes "one flesh." While he gives excellent counsel to both partners, we will here focus on the role of the priesthood bearer. Husbands are told to love their wives. How is that to be accomplished? "As Christ loved the Church." How did Christ love the Church, his bride? He sanctified and cleansed it through his own selfless sacrifice. He gave his life for his bride so she could be presented to him without blemish—glorious and beautiful. All that Christ did was directed to the glorification and edification of his bride.

It is easy to see how perfectly this coincides with the overall function of the priesthood. Remember, Melchizedek focused his work on leading his people to perfection and exaltation. That is the responsibility of a king of righteousness as he relates to his own bride. Husbands are to treat their wives in such a manner that they may become holy, glorified, and perfect. After all, Paul teaches, the husband is going to present this perfect bride to himself; she is part of him. It should be natural for the husband to love his wife as fully as he loves himself and to seek to encourage and help her to be as perfect as she can be. And all this is to be done in the same patient, loving, gentle, and uncritical manner in which Christ sought to perfect his disciples.

Nourish and Cherish

Paul then offers two excellent terms describing the method a husband should use in building and edifying his wife: *nourisheth* and *cherisheth*. What nourishes another person? Does impatience, bullying, criticism, apathy, or harshness nourish? Or is a person better nourished by love, gentleness, meekness, and patience? In the scriptures the word *nourish* is frequently tied in meaning to the gospel. We are constantly in need of being nourished spiritually. Did not the Savior nourish his bride with his teachings, example, and Spirit? We can easily see the relationship of nourishing to all the priesthood represents. A wife who is nourished by the priesthood bearer will find happiness, peace, and rest in her husband's righteousness. She can willingly follow him as he follows the Savior, and they will both become more and more like our Father in Heaven.

Cherish connotes tenderness, mercy, and sacred love. It suggests reverence and honor. A husband who cherishes his wife places her in a position of value and importance. He would never belittle her or cause her to doubt her position of oneness with him. She would know that no other person or thing takes precedence in his mind. President Kimball gives us a wonderful example of what it means to cherish a marriage partner:

> The Lord says in no uncertain terms: "Thou shalt love thy wife with all thy heart, and shalt cleave unto her and none else" (D&C 42:22).
>
> And, when the Lord says *all* thy heart, it allows for no sharing nor dividing nor depriving. . . .
>
> The words *none else* eliminate everyone and everything. The spouse then becomes preeminent in the life of the husband or wife, and neither social life nor occupa-

tional life nor political life nor any other interest nor person nor thing shall ever take precedence over the companion spouse. . . .

Marriage presupposes total allegiance and total fidelity. Each spouse takes the partner with the understanding that he or she gives totally to the spouse all the heart, strength, loyalty, honor, and affection, with all dignity. Any divergence is sin; any sharing of the heart is transgression. As we should have "an eye single to the glory of God," so should we have an eye, an ear, a heart single to the marriage and the spouse and family. (Spencer W. Kimball, *Faith Precedes the Miracle* [Salt Lake City: Deseret Book Co., 1972], pp. 142–43.)

How completely foreign to so much of the world's views of men and women is the priesthood's vision of marriage! Sadly, too many priesthood bearers "rule" in their homes rather than nourish and cherish. Did not Christ teach that he who would be great must be the servant of all? Did he not give a perfect example of this when he washed his disciples' feet? Christ served his bride in true love and meekness. A king of righteousness should strive to serve his wife in that same spirit.

The Principles of Righteousness

Section 121 of the Doctrine and Covenants contains inspired writings of the Prophet Joseph Smith while he was a prisoner in Liberty Jail and deals in large part with the manner in which priesthood authority is controlled. The principles taught there apply to all priesthood responsibilities, but we will examine them in the context of a man's most critical apprenticeship—as husband and father. Joseph writes,

Behold, there are many called, but few are chosen. And why are they not chosen?

Because their hearts are set so much upon the things of this world, and aspire to the honors of men, that they do not learn this one lesson—

That the rights of the priesthood *are inseparably connected with the powers of heaven*, and that the powers of
heaven *cannot be controlled* nor handled *only upon the
principles of righteousness*. (D&C 121:34–36, italics added.)

The right of a husband to rule by virtue of his priesthood can
be handled only upon the principles of righteousness. In verses
that follow the above, Joseph Smith details those principles. He
teaches that priesthood may be conferred upon a man, but cov-
ering sins, gratifying pride or ambition, or exercising control or
compulsion on any other person in an unrighteous manner ends
the man's priesthood authority and grieves the Spirit. Often the
family is the scene of men's attempts to exercise dominion in
unrighteousness. The priesthood bearer should feel that he
leads in his home because he righteously exercises the priesthood and not merely because he is male. Cultivating this attitude is one of the best ways husbands can honor their priesthood responsibility to their wives. Righteous ruling in this
manner carries with it the approval of the Spirit.

However, righteous leadership is difficult for many men.
Joseph Smith continued: "We have learned by sad experience
that *it is the nature* and disposition of almost all men, *as soon as
they get a little authority, as they suppose*, they will immediately begin to exercise unrighteous dominion. Hence many are
called, but few are chosen." (D&C 121:39–40, italics added.)

The priesthood will help a man overcome this natural disposition if it is rightly understood. What a mockery to the Lord that
some husbands exercise unrighteous dominion in their homes in
the name of the priesthood! Such an unholy, impure practice
greatly offends God; indeed, we are told that "the Spirit of the
Lord is grieved" when unrighteous dominion is practiced (D&C
121:37).

Specific principles govern the righteous exercise of priesthood authority. "No power or influence can or ought to be
maintained by virtue of the priesthood," the scripture states,
"only by persuasion, by long-suffering, by gentleness and
meekness, and by love unfeigned; by kindness, and pure
knowledge, which shall greatly enlarge the soul without hypoc-

risy, and without guile'' (D&C 121:41–42). A key word in the passage is *maintained*. When a woman marries a priesthood holder in the temple, she has a natural desire to be nourished, cherished, and loved by her husband. That natural desire can be maintained only when her husband exhibits the characteristics given in the scriptures. Any other method will impair and perhaps eventually kill the relationship. An eternal marriage which carries with it the promises spoken of in Doctrine and Covenants 132 can be built upon no other principles.

A king of righteousness uses persuasion, not command; he is patient, not quick to condemn or correct; he is gentle and meek, not rough and haughty; his love is pure, not hypocritical, seeking selfish ends; he is kind, not thoughtless or cruel. In making significant decisions, he seeks the inspiration of the Lord, and he lives his life in such a way that he can receive ''pure knowledge.'' The Savior is the supreme example of all these traits. He applied them in ruling and guiding his Church. If a wife is nourished by these ''principles of righteousness,'' she will know that her husband's ''faithfulness is stronger than the cords of death'' (D&C 121:44). The children will also feel and know of their father's love and devotion to them.

Without Compulsory Means

Joseph Smith concludes this section of the Doctrine and Covenants with two beautiful verses about the priesthood.

> Let thy bowels also be full of charity towards all men, and to the household of faith, and let virtue garnish thy thoughts unceasingly; then shall thy confidence wax strong in the presence of God; and the doctrine of the priesthood shall distil upon thy soul as the dews from heaven.
>
> The Holy Ghost shall be thy constant companion, and thy scepter an unchanging scepter of righteousness and truth; and thy dominion shall be an everlasting dominion, and without compulsory means it shall flow unto thee forever and ever. (D&C 121:45–46.)

These two verses need but little commentary. The promise of increased confidence before God, clearer understanding of the doctrines of the priesthood, and the constant affiliation of the Holy Ghost are all significant and necessary to becoming a king of righteousness. The importance of charity and virtuous thought is also self-explanatory, particularly in a world where virtue is so often negated.

We might note one or two thoughts arising from verse 46. Remember that a righteous Melchizedek Priesthood bearer, by the significance of the name Melchizedek, desires to be a king. A king holds a scepter, a token of the king's right to rule. The promise is therefore given that the husband or father who rules according to the "principles of righteousness" outlined in verses 41 and 42 will hold his "scepter" constantly, without change. His kingdom will endure through the eternities.

A king has a domain over which he rules. The faithful priesthood holder is promised that his "dominion" will be an "everlasting dominion" if he righteously applies the principles outlined in verses 41 and 42. The last lines of verse 46 are very beautiful when thought of in context of a wife. A wife's love will "flow" to the husband forever and ever. It will flow without "compulsory means" as naturally as it did when they knelt at the altar in the temple, but it will be intensified by a lifetime of "gentleness," "meekness," "kindness," and "unfeigned love." In these marriages compulsion is unnecessary and foreign.

This last phrase in verse 46 helps us understand the true meaning of the Lord's words to Eve in the Garden of Eden just after she and Adam partook of the fruit. He told her, "Thy *desire* shall be to thy husband, and he shall rule over thee" (Moses 4:22, italics added). The key word in this phrase is not "rule," but "desire." What righteous wife would not desire and love a man who treated her according to the principles of righteousness inherent in the priesthood? If a husband does not believe that his wife's "desire" flows to him without compulsion, the answer is not greater compulsion or authority but a clearer understanding of what it means to be a prince of peace, a king of righteousness, a bearer of the Melchizedek Priesthood. The responsibility for improving their relationship often lies with himself and the manner in which he exercises that priesthood.

The King of Righteousness as a Father

The second familial relationship that is critical to the priesthood is the father-child relationship. Before a man can become a "father of many nations" in the eternal sense of that phrase, he must prove to God that he can be a righteous father of his own earthly children. Then he that is faithful over a few things may be made ruler over many things.

A brief reflection on the truths taught in Doctrine and Covenants 121 reveals that the scriptural "principles of righteousness" apply to children as well. A father will "maintain" his child's love and honor only if he treats that child with gentleness, persuasion, meekness, and unfeigned love. Children are in turn commanded of the Lord to "honor" their fathers. *Honor* is a word with many meanings. It was well chosen, for it encompasses respect, trust, obedience, reverence, giving glory, and so on. To help his child to truly honor him, however, the father should be worthy of that honor. The most clear example of this relationship is that of the Father and the Son. Christ honored the Father in every sense of the word, and the Father was certainly worthy of that devotion.

Father As Teacher

If a child's primary duty is to honor, what is the primary duty of the father? It is to *teach*. This is clearly defined throughout the scriptures. Not only do the scriptures command a father to teach his children but they are also very specific about the truths he should teach. Let us examine a few.

And again, inasmuch as parents have children in Zion, or in any of her stakes which are organized, that teach them not to understand the doctrine of repentance, faith in Christ the Son of the living God, and of baptism and the gift of the Holy Ghost by the laying on of the hands, when eight years old, the sin be upon the heads of the parents.

For this shall be a law unto the inhabitants of Zion, or in any of her stakes which are organized. . . .

And they shall also teach their children to pray, and to walk uprightly before the Lord. . . .

Now, I, the Lord, am not well pleased with the inhabitants of Zion, for there are idlers among them; and their children are also growing up in wickedness; they also seek not earnestly the riches of eternity, but their eyes are full of greediness. (D&C 68:25–26, 28, 31.)

In these verses parents are instructed to teach their children to understand several basic doctrines and principles:

1. Faith in Christ.
2. Repentance.
3. Baptism.
4. The gift of the Holy Ghost.
5. Prayer.
6. Walking uprightly before the Lord.
7. Working and seeking for the riches of eternity.

Parents sin when they fail to teach their children these principles. To properly teach a child the principles requires more than a few family home evening lessons; it requires years of instruction, example being the best method. It is here that the partnership help of a righteous wife becomes critical.

For a child to properly understand the above principles will require that he learn other knowledge as well. A child must know Christ. A child must learn the life and teachings of the Savior in order to have true faith in him. He must know right and wrong and be somewhat aware of the consequences of sin before repentance can become a force in his life. Eventually he must learn of the Atonement and of the relationship of justice and mercy. This knowledge brings understanding to both repentance and baptism and will certainly increase faith in Christ. A child must understand what a covenant is, including the specific covenants of baptism and the sacrament. Parents must help each child understand not only who the Holy Ghost is and what he does but also how to listen for him and how to know when the still, small voice is speaking. A child must love and have faith in our Father in Heaven before the child can earnestly seek him in prayer. A child also wants to know how to get answers to his prayers. A knowledge of the scriptures, the statements of the prophets, and the commandments of God are all vital to walking uprightly. Responsibility comes with work and proper values. Priorities and goals are instilled when a child learns to seek earnestly the riches of eternity. The applications of the scripture verses quoted above are limitless.

King Benjamin encourages parents to instill other values as well:

> And ye will not suffer your children that they go hungry, or naked; neither will ye suffer that they transgress the laws of God, and fight and quarrel one with another, and serve the devil, who is the master of sin, or who is the evil spirit which hath been spoken of by our fathers, he being an enemy to all righteousness.

> But ye will teach them to walk in the ways of truth and soberness; ye will teach them to love one another, and to serve one another. (Mosiah 4:14–15.)

If a priesthood holder is to be a prince of peace, then, he must teach his own family to live in peace with each other. Fighting, quarreling, and contention serve the adversary. Christ taught the Nephites that "he that hath the spirit of contention is not of me, but is of the devil" (3 Nephi 11:29). The father should set the example in this vital area, especially in his relationship with his wife. Children should learn to love and serve each other. Once again the father's example of love and service is critical. Children's "walk" and daily activities should follow the path of truthfulness. King Benjamin also mentions soberness. This trait refers to a person's serious understanding of the importance of life and his respect for the commandments of God.

These are but a few verses that speak of the critical things a father and mother are to teach together. Children come into the world innocent and clean; much of their success in life will depend on the foundation they are given while young. Notice the clear-cut responsibility placed on fathers in the following verses:

> But behold, I say unto you, that little children are redeemed from the foundation of the world through mine Only Begotten;

Wherefore, they cannot sin, for power is not given unto Satan to tempt little children, until they begin to become accountable before me;

For it is given unto them even as I will, according to mine own pleasure, *that great things may be required at the hand of their fathers* (D&C 29:46–48, italics added).

Stir Up a Child to Feel After God

In presenting the *Lectures on Faith*, the Prophet Joseph Smith spoke of the great patriarchs in the early ages of the world and gave a wonderful summation of the full responsibility of a father to his child. Though his topic was faith rather than the priesthood role of fathers, the advice is sound and the tie with the priesthood apparent:

The existence of God became an object of faith in the early age of the world. And the evidences which these men had of the existence of a God, *was the testimony of their fathers* in the first instance.

The reason why we have been thus particular on this part of our subject, is that this class may see by what means it was that God became an object of faith among men after the fall; and what it was that stirred up the faith of multitudes to feel after him—to search after a knowledge of his character, perfections and attributes, until they became extensively acquainted with him, and not only commune with him and behold his glory, but be partakers of his power and stand in his presence. . . .

. . . We have seen that it was human testimony, and human testimony only, that excited this inquiry, in the first instance, in their minds. It was the credence they gave to the testimony of their fathers, this testimony having aroused their minds to inquire after the knowledge of God. . . .

. . . And after they were made acquainted with his existence, by the testimony of their father, they were dependent upon the exercise of their own faith, for a knowledge of his character. (*Lectures on Faith*, 2:33–35, 56, italics added.)

The primary duty of an honorable Melchizedek Priesthood father who magnifies his calling as a father is to "stir" up his children to "feel" after God; to cause his children to "search" after a knowledge of God's character; to "excite" his children to inquire; and to "arouse" his children's minds to know God.

Joseph Smith stated that human testimony excites this inquiring. Therefore, children should often hear their father's and their mother's testimony and conviction. All the counsels given by Benjamin in Mosiah chapter 4 and by the Lord in Doctrine and Covenants section 68 point to this overall objective. Once parents have excited this inquiry in their children and turned them to God the Eternal Father, the children can become partakers of God's power and glory. They then become responsible for exercising their own faith.

Raised in Light and Truth

The scriptures give added counsel on this necessary function of a righteous patriarch. Parents are to begin to teach children important truths early in life. The Apostle Paul describes the latter-day world in very graphic terms: "In the last days perilous times shall come," he warned. "For men shall be lovers of their own selves, covetous, boasters, proud, blasphemers, disobedient to parents, unthankful, unholy, without natural affection, trucebreakers, false accusers, incontinent, fierce, despisers of those that are good, traitors, heady, highminded, lovers of pleasures more than lovers of God" (2 Timothy 3:1–4). Then Paul gives to Timothy a key to living in that world and remaining unspotted by reminding him "that from a child thou hast known the holy scriptures, which are able to make thee wise unto salvation through faith which is in Christ Jesus" (2 Timothy 3:15). A son or daughter should strive to learn "from a child" to love the holy scriptures. In so doing, he or she will find the wisdom and the faith to resist temptation and worldliness.

In Doctrine and Covenants 93 the Lord gives similar advice to all parents: "But I have commanded you to bring up your children in light and truth" (D&C 93:40).

Children should never need to stumble because their parents failed to keep them in the light. The concept of not teaching religious and moral values and principles until children are "old enough to decide for themselves" is a device of the adversary. The Lord expects parents to acquaint their children with light and truth from the very beginning years. Then children will know the difference between light and dark, truth and error, good and evil. They will know because they have tasted the good, the true and the lovely, and can make comparisons. How can parents expect children to shun the influences of inappropriate modern music and unwholesome entertainments when they have never been shown their truly "virtuous," "lovely," or "praiseworthy" counterparts? Let the best music, literature, movies, and art surround children when they are young, and these arts will tend to cultivate an expectation and a search for that which is commendable and worthy rather than that which is degrading and prevalent in the ever-changing youth cultures of the day.

The command to "bring up your children in light and truth" given in section 93 is followed by exhortations to four presiding members of the Lord's restored kingdom—Frederick G. Williams, Sidney Rigdon, Joseph Smith, and Newel K. Whitney. All these leaders were under condemnation for failing to fulfill the commandment to teach their families light and truth.

To Frederick G. Williams the Lord commanded, "You have not taught your children light and truth, according to the commandments; and that wicked one hath power, as yet, over you, and this is the cause of your affliction" (D&C 93:42). The Lord then told him how to remove his "affliction." "And now a commandment I give unto you—if you will be delivered you shall *set in order your own house*, for there are many things that are not right in your house" (D&C 93:43, italics added). Similar counsel was given to Sidney Rigdon: "In some things he hath not kept the commandments concerning his children; therefore, *first set in order thy house*" (D&C 93:44, italics added).

The word *first* is very significant. At the time, these men constituted the First Presidency and Presiding Bishop. In spite of the very important work of the kingdom they were engaged in, the responsibility to be a king of righteousness to their children came "first," as it always has in the Church.

Joseph Smith is told: "And now, verily I say unto Joseph Smith, Jun.—You have not kept the commandments, and must needs stand rebuked before the Lord; your family must needs repent and forsake some things, and give more earnest heed unto your sayings, or be removed out of their place" (D&C 93:47–48). After these rebukes the Lord enlarged his counsel to include all priesthood fathers by saying, "What I say unto one I say unto all" (D&C 93:49).

The Lord then chastened Newel K. Whitney, telling him to "set in order his family, and see that they are more diligent and concerned at home, and pray always, or they shall be removed out of their place" (D&C 93:50). These rebukes are plain to understand. In the Lord's mind an LDS father is obligated to teach his children light and truth. To fail to do so is to bring upon himself and his family the condemnation of our Father in Heaven, not to mention the inevitable sorrows that will come to children who are not acquainted with that light and truth.

A Father's Influence

No one can judge the depth of a righteous father's influence on his children. The Book of Mormon is especially strong on this point. A brief examination of several leading characters will reveal the strong influences of a righteous father on his sons. While some children failed to follow good examples, as in the case of Laman and Lemuel, the majority of relationships are positive.

Nephi is given his great vision of the tree of life because his father has stirred up his heart to ponder the vision his father saw. While pondering he is "caught away in the Spirit of the Lord." "What desirest thou?" an angel asks Nephi. "I desire to behold the things which my father saw." He is then asked if he believes his father, to which Nephi replies, "Yea, thou knowest that I believe all the words of my father." (1 Nephi 11:1–5.)

Lehi's influence is also easily seen on his firstborn son in the wilderness. Jacob's words and teachings on the Atonement, found in 2 Nephi 9, are profoundly influenced by and built upon his father's final blessing to him, found in 2 Nephi 2.

Jacob, in his own right, caused his son Enos to "feel after" God. Enos relates that while hunting beasts in the forest "the words which I had often heard my father speak concerning eternal life, and the joy of the saints, sunk deep into my heart" (Enos 1:3). Jacob was not a casual father. He "often" spoke to his son. His teachings were apparently positive. He spoke of the "joy of the saints." Reflecting on his father's influence, Enos also states, "I, Enos, knowing my father that he was a just man —for he taught me . . . in the *nurture and admonition* of the Lord—and blessed be the name of my God for it" (Enos 1:1, italics added). *Nurture* is a powerful word. It connotes a loving relationship. Enos was carefully fed the truths of life. He was taught the joys of the saints as well as the admonitions or commandments of the Lord. Both are necessary and help a child "feel" after God.

King Benjamin's three sons, one of whom would become King Mosiah, were "taught in all the language of his fathers, that thereby they might become men of understanding; and that they might know concerning the prophecies. . . . And he also taught them concerning the records which were engraven on the plates of brass." (Mosiah 1:2–3.) Later Mosiah's own sons received his blessing and assurance of safety as they departed to preach to the Lamanites.

We often attribute Alma the Younger's quick repentance to the prayers of his father, but it was also his father's teachings on Christ that prompted Alma to "feel after" God. "And it came to pass that as I was thus racked with torment, while I was harrowed up by the memory of my many sins, behold, *I remembered also to have heard my father prophesy* unto the people concerning the coming of one Jesus Christ, a Son of God, to atone for the sins of the world" (Alma 36:17, italics added). Undoubtedly Alma, like Enos, "often" heard these teachings. In his moment of crisis and need, the teaching and prophesying of his father came to his mind.

Corianton, Alma's wayward son, was in his turn saved from his rebellion and his excuses by Alma's gentle but firm insight into his son's problems. Alma obviously knew his son very well, for he frequently probed his son's anxieties by saying, "I perceive that thy mind is worried" (Alma 40:1; see also 41:1), or "I perceive there is somewhat more which doth worry your mind" (Alma 42:1). What a beautiful example of the need for a father to truly understand the concerns and thoughts of his child, especially a wayward one!

Helaman, the son of Helaman, had a profound influence on his sons Nephi and Lehi, as recorded in Helaman 5. He gave his sons righteous names to live up to, and his teachings on the Savior filled their thoughts as they decided to spend a lifetime preaching the gospel while leaving behind worldly positions of power.

Mormon's influence on Moroni, implied in their correspondence, and Moroni's frequent inclusion of his father's words in his own concluding book, show their deep love and mutual confidence.

The list cannot be limited to the Book of Mormon. Even in the brief accounts found in the Pearl of Great Price we read of Enoch's gratitude for his father's teachings: "And he said unto them: I came out from the land of Cainan, the land of my fathers, a land of righteousness unto this day. And my father taught me in all the ways of God." (Moses 6:41.)

It is significant that even a brief overview of some of the great prophets reveals that they were great fathers also. One calling did not supersede the other, but perpetuated instead a line of honorable priesthood bearers who "were made acquainted with [God's] existence by the testimony of their father" and then "[communed] with him and [beheld] his glory" (*Lectures on Faith*, 2:56, 35).

Many daughters have done virtuously, but
thou excellest them all. Favour is deceitful,
and beauty is vain: but a woman that feareth
the Lord, she shall be praised. Give her of the
fruit of her hands; and let her own works
praise her in the gates.
                            —Proverbs 31:29–31

CHAPTER THREE

An Elect
Lady

If a husband is to "present to himself a glorious" wife (see chapter 2 under "Maintaining a Oneness"), it might be helpful for
him to know some of the scriptural descriptions of a noble and
righteous woman. Some men have the wrong picture in their
minds of what a wife is expected to do or be. Many women also
have various and often conflicting views of what the ideal Latter-
day Saint wife should be like. An examination of the scriptures
should help both husbands and wives develop the proper per-
spectives. In presenting these ideas I do not wish to give the impression that this is what a priesthood holder should demand of
his wife. Rather these are some areas in which a loving husband
can encourage and praise his wife.

A priesthood-bearing husband should regularly ask himself,
What can I do to help my wife "reverence" (Ephesians 5:33)
and honor my priesthood, with its accompanying role of husband and father? The answer, of course, would be to live the
principles of righteousness detailed in Ephesians 5 and Doctrine
and Covenants 121. The proper attitude for a wife would also
focus on self-improvement.

She would concentrate on those areas that would help her husband to love, cherish, and honor her. Many of those principles are given in Doctrine and Covenants 25. In this section, the Lord calls Emma Smith "an elect lady." The last verse indicates that the counsel given in this section to Emma is meant to be applied to all LDS women who would become "elect" ladies. The Lord explains, "And verily, verily, I say unto you, that this is my voice unto all. Amen." (D&C 25:16.)

The Paths of Virtue

Section 25 contains a number of descriptions that will help an honorable priesthood bearer know what his Father in Heaven values in his daughters. First, Emma is told to be "faithful and walk in the paths of virtue before me." The word *virtue* has many connotations, all of which can help us to understand what the path of virtue is. It certainly implies the honoring and obeying of the law of chastity, both before and after marriage. Furthermore, it implies an attitude of purity held by both husband and wife toward the procreative gift given by God to man. This is beautifully expressed by Mormon as "that which was most dear and precious above all things, which is chastity and virtue" (Moroni 9:9). A husband who is concerned about his wife's "most precious" possession will not seek to degrade or compromise her in any manner, either before or after marriage.

Aside from the connotation of chastity and purity, another connotation of virtue can be found in the thirteenth article of faith: "If there is anything virtuous, lovely, or of good report or praiseworthy, we seek after these things." Walking in the paths of virtue means seeking the best, the highest, and the most praiseworthy things of life. This includes the finest literature, entertainment, music, and art. Husbands should encourage their wives in the pursuit of virtues of this type. The thirteenth article indicates that pursuit is active; we are to "seek" these things. Indeed, we would do well to govern all our activities by the principles outlined in the thirteenth article of faith.

The Old Testament gives a few more insights on the paths of virtue. Boaz describes Ruth as "a virtuous woman" (Ruth 3:11). Not only does Boaz believe this of Ruth but also "all the city of my people doth know" she is virtuous. Ruth's life was filled with compassion, selflessness, loyalty, and industry. These mark the paths of virtue, as does the description of "a virtuous woman" in the last chapter of Proverbs. In this chapter such a woman is described as having a price "far above rubies" (Proverbs 31:10). This is followed by a description of the industry, loyalty, and wisdom inherent in her life. The last verses are very beautiful and constitute the praise a husband or father would give to his wife or daughter as she walks in the paths of virtue: "Many daughters have done virtuously, but thou excellest them all. Favour is deceitful, and beauty is vain: but a woman that feareth the Lord, she shall be praised." (Proverbs 31:29–30.)

Emma was counseled to walk in the path of virtue before the Lord. This corresponds perfectly with the description in Proverbs of a virtuous woman fearing (that is, respecting, honoring, and loving) the Lord. The emphasis is not only on her relationship to her husband or children. She walks virtue's paths, for this is the way she honors her Father in Heaven. Each husband and father should so guide his actions that his wife and daughters honor their Father in Heaven.

It should also be pointed out that virtue was one of the principles of righteousness required of men. Remember that Joseph Smith encouraged a priesthood holder to "let virtue garnish thy thoughts unceasingly" (D&C 121:45). The Lord requires obedience to his commandments of both men and women—no one is exempt based on gender alone. The man, as head of the home, should set the example of virtuous living. Then his wife and children will be more willing to follow his example.

The Spirit of Meekness

Emma was next counseled to be "a comfort unto my servant, Joseph Smith, Jun., thy husband, in his afflictions, with consoling words, in the spirit of meekness. And thou shalt go with him at the time of his going, and be unto him for a scribe, while there is no one to be a scribe for him." (D&C 25:5–6.) These verses need little commentary. They are a very good definition of what it means to be a "help meet" for someone. Meekness is a trait expected of men, as we saw in Doctrine and Covenants 121. The man should once again set an example by acquiring a meek attitude and behavior. A wife who seeks to honor her husband and cultivate a oneness will recognize her husband's need for consolation and counsel. Oneness is also implied by the counsel to "go with him at the time of his going." Emma was intimately involved in helping Joseph fulfill his calling. At this time that involved acting as a scribe. Emma supported Joseph's activities and in turn was blessed by her husband. An elect lady, therefore, supports her husband; she "goes with him" and sustains him in his various responsibilities both in and out of the Church.

Learning Much

The Lord then tells Emma: "And thou shalt be ordained under his hand to expound scriptures, and to exhort the church, according as it shall be given thee by my Spirit. For he shall lay his hands upon thee, and thou shalt receive the Holy Ghost, and thy time shall be given to writing, and to learning much." (D&C 25:7-8.)

One central thought seems to be implied here—Emma is to improve her mind, specifically as it concerns the scriptures and revelations of God. An elect lady should be able to expound on and to exhort the membership of the Church in the scriptures. This is certainly true in regard to her own children. She has a right to and should seek the influence of the Spirit. A true son of Abraham will help to cultivate these qualities in his wife.

It is interesting that the words *expound* and *exhort* are the identical words given in section 20 as responsibilities of the priesthood. We can see a pattern developing in the repeated application of certain principles to both husbands and wives. Both men and women are to practice virtue, meekness, and so on. In this way a woman becomes one with her husband, and both share in the blessings of the priesthood.

As if to place a capstone on this principle of growth in knowledge, particularly revelatory knowledge, the Lord tells Emma to devote her time to "learning much." This certainly includes the scriptures, for without learning the truths contained therein, no one can be effective in exhorting or expounding. However, "learning much" may be broadened to include all truth. In a later section of the Doctrine and Covenants the Lord gives his children a commandment to "teach one another the doctrine of the kingdom" (D&C 88:77), and then expands that commandment to include all worthy learning. We are to study "things both in heaven and in the earth, and under the earth; things which have been, things which are, things which must shortly come to pass; things which are at home, things which are abroad; the wars and the perplexities of the nations, and the judgments which are on the land; and a knowledge also of countries and of kingdoms" (D&C 88:79).

We are told that "the glory of God is intelligence" (D&C 93:36) and are exhorted to seek "out of the best books words of wisdom [and] learning" (D&C 88:118). The scriptures and statements of the prophets are filled with encouragement to improve our minds in order to serve and love God with all of our hearts, minds, and strength (see Mark 12:30). Every righteous priesthood holder should encourage his wife to develop her mind through studying the scriptures and other noble areas of knowledge. This can help considerably in the wife's challenging task of raising children in righteousness and will also assist her to have a fuller life.

These principles correspond perfectly with walking in the paths of virtue as virtue is explained in the thirteenth article of faith. Good, lovely, praiseworthy learning is encouraged. This may follow the pathways of art, literature, science, history, homemaking skills, or any of a hundred different pursuits. Once again the role of the priesthood holder is to set an example by constantly developing his own mind and expanding his learning, particularly of the scriptures. Learning includes using and developing talents. In Emma's case, she was encouraged to use her knowledge of music in selecting hymns for the Church. An elect lady develops her talents in order to be a more effective tool in the Lord's hand for strengthening and supporting his kingdom on the earth.

Seek the Things of a Better World

Emma is told in verse 9 that she "[need] not fear, for thy husband shall support thee." This was the Lord's assurance to Emma that Joseph would be the "bread winner" in their home even though his time and occupation were dedicated to the Church. A wife can righteously expect that her husband will support her that she might fulfill, without hindrance, her vital role as mother. The Lord made this point very clear in another revelation: "Women have claim on their husbands for their maintenance, until their husbands are taken" (D&C 83:2). Husbands and wives need to realize the importance of this counsel. It is immediately followed by a general statement of principle which governs the life of an elect lady. "And verily I say unto thee that thou shalt lay aside the things of this world, and seek for the things of a better" (D&C 25:10). This principle may from time to time require sacrifice. It is certainly the spirit of modern-day prophets' counsel for mothers to remain in the home rather than seek occupation elsewhere. However, there may be choices a family will need to make while trying to lay aside the things of this world. This is certainly applicable counsel to the priesthood holder. We can gain a little more insight into this issue by examining other verses that relate to it.

In Doctrine and Covenants 30 David Whitmer is told "Your mind has been on the things of the earth more than on the things of me, your Maker" (D&C 30:2). "Laying aside the things of the world" often requires a change in the desires of the mind and heart. The Lord desires a singleness of heart and purpose. The things of God must be more important to us than the things of the world. Emma is counseled to "seek for the things of a better" world, just as David Whitmer is counseled to place his mind on the things of God. There is action and pursuit involved in the word *seek*. It is directly associated with some of the covenants made in the temple, where we commit to actively support God's kingdom. The elect lady builds the kingdom of God in her own life, in the life of her family, and in the broader society.

The new edition of the LDS scriptures provides an interesting cross-reference to Doctrine and Covenants 25:10. A fuller meaning to seeking the things of a better world is gained by examining this additional scripture:

Wherefore, whoso believeth in God might with surety hope for a better world, yea, even a place at the right hand of God, which hope cometh of faith, maketh an anchor to the souls of men, which would make them sure and steadfast, always abounding in good works, being led to glorify God (Ether 12:4).

Seeking the things of God involves "good works" that will glorify God. These works should be "steadfast" and "sure." The husband who holds the Melchizedek Priesthood will do all he can to help his wife be worthy to *inherit* a "better world" and also to *build* a better world during this temporal existence. Notice again the similarity in the roles of the Melchizedek Priesthood bearer and his wife who seeks to support and honor that priesthood.

Rejoice

After asking Emma to make a collection of hymns, the Lord instructs, "Lift up thy heart and rejoice" (D&C 25:13). On the surface this may appear insignificant, but with a little thought the importance of this counsel becomes apparent. The scriptures are filled with references to cheerfulness, joy, and happiness. The Lord constantly exhorts his people to lift up their heads and to be of good cheer. One of the very best examples of the need to rejoice is given in 2 Nephi 4, in which Nephi records his thoughts after the death of his father, Lehi. He senses that Lehi's death and his brothers' plotting will lead to the separation of the family. These thoughts and the afflictions he has suffered over the years create in him a great sorrow and depression. Perhaps Nephi also feels a little sorry for himself. Speaking of this moment Nephi records, "O then, if I have seen so great things, if the Lord in his condescension unto the children of men hath visited men in so much mercy, why should my heart weep and my soul linger in the valley of sorrow, and my flesh waste away, and my strength slacken, because of mine afflictions?" (2 Nephi 4:26.)

Depression and sorrow are common emotions, but people should not "linger" in that valley, especially Latter-day Saints to whom so much has been given. Nephi's response to his sorrow is a recounting of his past experiences with the Lord. This is why he states, "If the Lord in his condescension unto the children of men hath visited men in so much mercy, why should my heart weep?" The realization of God's mercy and goodness caused Nephi to say, "Rejoice, O my heart, and give place no more for the enemy of my soul. . . . Rejoice, O my heart, and cry unto the Lord." (2 Nephi 4:28, 30.) Nephi considers his lingering in the valley of sorrow a sign of ingratitude to the Lord, and as he ponders his blessings he admonishes himself to rejoice.

There is great truth in this attitude. No people on the face of this earth have greater reason to "lift up [our hearts] and rejoice" than do we. We have been given the knowledge, truths, covenants, powers, and blessings of the gospel. Aside from this we live in a time of scientific advancement and a country of political freedoms. Our blessings are countless. For us to remain in a state of depression, sorrow, or moodiness is a sign of our failure to appreciate the many reasons God has given us to rejoice. An elect lady recognizes this and "rejoices." Her attitude is positive, optimistic, and cheerful.

There will still be moments in life when we express our grief. Suffering is part of human existence and sorrow is sometimes an appropriate and meaningful emotion. However, a proper balance must be found if we are to lead emotionally healthy lives. Clues to that balance are discovered in the words Christ spoke to his disciples at the Last Supper.

At the Last Supper, Christ gave mankind the greatest reason to rejoice. As the Last Supper was concluded and the Savior contemplated his coming agony, he told his disciples the following:

> Behold, the hour cometh, yea, is now come, that ye shall be scattered, every man to his own, and shall leave me alone: and yet I am not alone, because the Father is with me.
>
> These things I have spoken unto you, that in me ye might have peace. In the world ye shall have tribulation: but be of good cheer; I have overcome the world. (John 16:32–33.)

The realization of Christ's ultimate victory over Satan and the world creates in each individual the hope spoken of in the scriptures. This knowledge caused Alma to say: "And then may God grant unto you that your burdens may be light, through the joy of his Son. And even all this can ye do if ye will. Amen." (Alma 33:23.)

These principles are not limited by gender. Every priesthood holder should lift up his head and rejoice in the knowledge that God has granted us, and in the blessings of the Atonement. Men of the priesthood have an obligation to teach their wives and children the joys of the gospel so that the family can cultivate an optimistic and grateful attitude. This attitude of joy was apparently a major portion of the key to Enos's conversion. As he hunted beasts in the forest he recalled his father's teachings, which centered on "the joy of the saints." This joy "sunk deep into my heart. And my soul hungered; and I kneeled down before my Maker." (Enos 1:3–4.)

The responsibility to provide a positive, cheerful outlook in a home rests on both the husband and the wife. Women who seek to honor the priesthood and become elect ladies, and men who strive to be kings of righteousness, will rejoice and provide an atmosphere of happiness and joy through the realization of the great gifts of God. That joy will survive even in the face of trial and hardship.

Cleave to the Covenants

In the same sentence wherein the Lord invites Emma to rejoice, he also instructs her: "Cleave unto the covenants which thou hast made" (D&C 25:13). It is fitting that this instruction would be given in the same sentence. True happiness and joy come not only from receiving blessings but also from the knowledge that one's life is in accordance with the will of God. Where there is guilt or sin, there is no real joy. Righteousness, which comes through faithfulness to our covenants, produces joy. By this standard, Christ, although a man "acquainted with grief," was the most joyful man ever to walk the earth, for he always did that which pleased the Father (see John 8:29). Moroni taught that "if ye have no hope ye must needs be in despair; and despair cometh because of iniquity" (Moroni 10:22). Lehi was contemplating these same principles when he taught Jacob:

"And if there be no righteousness there be no happiness" (2 Nephi 2:13).

To truly lift up one's heart and rejoice, one must "cleave unto the covenants." These covenants begin with baptism and the renewal of the sacrament. They include the temple endowment, marriage covenants, and all other covenants given and implied in the scriptures. A true son of Abraham will help his wife cleave unto her covenants so she might rejoice and have confidence in her Father in Heaven.

Delight in Thy Husband

Emma is then encouraged to "continue in the spirit of meekness, and beware of pride. Let thy soul delight in thy husband, and the glory which shall come upon him." (D&C 25:14.)

We have already commented on meekness. It is the antithesis of pride. Pride destroys marriages. It breaks the oneness that is needed. There should be no competition in a marriage relationship. All the honor that comes upon one partner comes upon the other. Emma is told to "delight" in her husband. She was to eliminate all feelings of jealousy for the "glory" of her husband, for they are the result of false pride.

This is excellent counsel today, as we see an increasing competition between husbands and wives. The elect lady will "delight" in her husband's priesthood, for she is the recipient of its greatest blessings. The priesthood bearer will not allow himself to be part of a power struggle. A wife's "delight" helps a man magnify his callings as husband, father, bishop, home teacher, and so on. Husbands should, however, help their wives "delight" in their "glory" by including them, counseling with them, and sharing with them in every worthy and righteous way. In this manner a wife will feel a part of her husband's work and calling, whether this work be secular or part of his priesthood calling.

It is equally as important in today's world that men also "delight" in every worthy accomplishment of their wives. Priesthood holders who make their wives' endeavors and callings subservient to their own exercise unrighteous dominion and undermine the oneness of their marriage.

The Crown of Righteousness

The Lord's concluding counsel to Emma is an exhortation to "keep my commandments continually, and a crown of righteousness thou shalt receive. And except thou do this, where I am you cannot come." (D&C 25:15.) The call to keep the commandments needs no commentary. Keeping God's commandments is the best way to honor the priesthood. Emma is promised that if she does this continually, a crown awaits her—she will become a queen. It is important to notice that the section of the Doctrine and Covenants directed to elect ladies ends with a similar promise to that given in section 121 to priesthood holders. Section 121 ends with the promise of an "unchanging scepter" and an "everlasting dominion." As the man becomes a king, so his wife, standing by his side, becomes a queen, wearing her crown of righteousness forever. In this eternal relationship they both honor the Father, and together they form an everlasting unit, receiving the blessing of eternal lives. That is why the Lord closes this counsel by saying "except thou do this, where I am you cannot come." God, as a celestial, glorified being, lives the laws he asks others to live. His children who seek to become kings and queens must follow eternal, unchanging example if they are to live where he lives.

Patience in Progression

Section 25 is not the only scripture that teaches these principles, nor does it include all principles necessary for a woman to follow to honor the priesthood, but it does contain the central principles. Honoring the priesthood for a woman does not necessarily mean strict obedience to a husband, especially if his rule is an unrighteous one. It does, however, mean striving to become an elect lady. When husbands and wives honor the principles of righteousness as they are given in sections 25 and 121 of the Doctrine and Covenants, they will become one and both will honor and magnify the priesthood.

Since living these lofty principles is not attained easily, the husband and the wife should both be patient, charitable, forgiving, and encouraging with each other. Neither one will be a perfect king or queen of righteousness immediately. As God is pleased with every positive step we make, let us also be pleased and build each other up. Above all, let both the husband and the wife cultivate an attitude that says, ''I can best help my companion to live his or her commitments by living *my own* as well as I can.'' A husband helps his wife love and delight in him most by living the principles of section 121. A wife helps her husband love and cherish her most by living the principles of section 25. With patience both can progress and become a king or queen of righteousness.

And again, he quoted the fifth verse thus: Behold, I will reveal unto you the Priesthood,
by the hand of Elijah the prophet, before the
coming of the great and dreadful day of the
Lord. He also quoted the next verse different-
ly: And *he shall plant in the hearts of the*
children the promises made to the fathers,
and the hearts of the children shall turn to
their fathers. If it were not so, the whole
earth would be utterly wasted at his coming.

—Joseph Smith—History 1:28-39

CHAPTER FOUR

The Abrahamic Covenant

We have shown the critical position a Melchizedek Priesthood
holder occupies in relation to his wife and children. This is his
most important kingdom. It is here that he can promote happiness, peace, and rest in order to prove himself worthy of eternal
increase. However, truly magnifying the priesthood carries with
it other responsibilities concerning the world and all God's
children. Now we will consider the priesthood as it correlates
with the Abrahamic covenant. This may help us gain an im-
proved understanding of (1) the importance of lineages pronounced in patriarchal blessings; (2) the expression "seed of
Abraham" as found in the oath and covenant of the priesthood;
and (3) the priesthood responsibility to the world.

An Elect People

God promised Abraham that his seed would be an elect and
a chosen people. The words *elect* and *chosen* refer to a certain

responsibility. Abraham's seed were elected to service. They were chosen to perform an assignment. The Savior explained this to the Nephites:

> And behold, ye are the children of the prophets; and ye are of the house of Israel; and ye are of the covenant which the Father made with your fathers, saying unto Abraham: *And in thy seed shall all the kindreds of the earth be blessed.*
>
> The Father having raised me up unto you first, and sent me to bless you in turning away every one of you from his iniquities; and this because ye are the children of the covenant—
>
> And after that ye were blessed then fulfilleth the Father the covenant which he made with Abraham, saying: In thy seed shall all the kindreds of the earth be blessed. (3 Nephi 20:25-27, italics added.)

Every covenant contains promises and blessings. The Lord promised Abraham that his seed would be granted the blessings of the gospel. In the above verses the Savior told the Nephites, who were a part of covenant Israel, that he would "bless" them by "turning away every one of you from his iniquities." This is a wonderful promise. What turns people from their iniquities, whether it be Old Testament Israelites, Book of Mormon Nephites, or Latter-day Saints? Only the principles of truth and righteousness contained in the gospel can keep a society or an individual righteous. And righteousness is the only means to happiness, peace, and rest.

Therefore to Abraham's seed went the most precious gifts of God. They were given prophets; they were given the priesthood and its accompanying ordinances, including the all-important gift of the Holy Ghost. They were given scriptures, truth, and knowledge. They were given chosen and promised lands that would be protected as long as they remained righteous. Their children, born into this covenant, would share in all these blessings. If they obeyed the law of the gospel, these gifts would turn them from iniquity and bring them back to the Eternal Father. The promise was given that each succeeding generation would be privileged to have these gifts, if they lived worthy of them and fulfilled their part of the covenant. This was their birthright under the covenant.

All the Families of the Earth

It is important to remember that the people of Abraham were chosen and elected because they were to take on a vital responsibility. That responsibility is suggested in the most often quoted passage of the Abrahamic covenant: "In thy seed shall all the kindreds of the earth be blessed" (3 Nephi 20:27). The following verses from the promises given to Abraham in other scriptures show the importance of this promise: "And I will bless them that bless thee, and curse him that curseth thee: and *in thee shall all families of the earth be blessed*" (Genesis 12:3, italics added). "And this covenant I make, that *thy children may be known among all nations*" (JST, Genesis 17:9, italics added). "Seeing that Abraham shall surely become a great and mighty nation, and *all the nations of the earth shall be blessed in him?*" (Genesis 18:18, italics added.) "And I will make thy seed to multiply as the stars of heaven, and will give unto thy seed all these countries; and *in thy seed shall all the nations of the earth be blessed;* because that Abraham obeyed my voice, and kept my charge, my commandments, my statutes, and my laws" (Genesis 26:4–5, italics added). It is clear that Abraham's seed was elected and chosen to bless all the nations of the earth with the treasures of eternity that God bestowed on them.

A Melchizedek Priesthood bearer carries the responsibility to fulfill this charge because he is of the "seed of Abraham." This was plainly taught to Abraham in the Pearl of Great Price. Immediately after Abraham was saved from the idolatrous priests of Ur, the Lord gave him the commission to bless all the nations of the earth: "I will take thee, to put upon thee my name, even the Priesthood of thy father, and my power shall be over thee. . . . *But through thy ministry my name shall be known in the earth forever, for I am thy God.*" (Abraham 1:18–19, italics added.) The seed of Abraham are elected to make known the Lord's name forever. This ties in directly with the covenant of baptism and the sacrament, wherein followers take upon themselves the name of Christ and, through obedience to covenants and righteous living, make his "name known" throughout the earth. This same focus was given to Abraham later: "For I have purposed to take thee away out of Haran, and to *make of thee a minister to bear my name in a strange land* which I will give unto thy seed after thee for an everlasting possession, when they hearken to my voice" (Abraham 2:6, italics added).

Just before Abraham's removal to Canaan the Lord reemphasized his responsibility to bless all the nations. At this moment the Lord spoke of specific blessings to be carried to the world, and of their direct relationship to the priesthood:

> And I will make of thee a great nation, and I will bless thee above measure, and make thy name great among all nations, and thou shalt be a blessing unto thy seed after thee, that in their hands *they shall bear this ministry and Priesthood unto all nations;*
>
> And I will bless them through thy name; for as many as receive this Gospel shall be called after thy name, and shall be accounted thy seed, and shall rise up and bless thee, as their father;
>
> And I will bless them that bless thee, and curse them that curse thee; and in thee *(that is, in thy Priesthood) and in thy seed (that is, thy Priesthood)*, for I give unto thee a promise that this right shall continue in thee, and in thy seed after thee (that is to say, the literal seed, or the seed of the body) *shall all the families of the earth be blessed, even with the blessings of the Gospel, which are the blessings of salvation, even of life eternal* (Abraham 2:9–11, italics added).

It is plain in this last scripture that the priesthood bearer is under covenant to share with the world the blessings he has received. He must "bear this ministry and priesthood" to all nations so that all nations may be blessed with the gospel, salvation, and life eternal. Only in this way can all God's children be "turned from [their] iniquities" and enjoy happiness, peace, and rest. These responsibilities under the direction of the priesthood apply to all Church members and constitute a major mission of the Lord's kingdom.

As if to impress upon us the need to preach the gospel, we are told a few verses later that Abraham was not idle with this responsibility as he traveled to the promised land: when he left for Canaan he took with him "the souls that we had won in Haran" (Abraham 2:15).

It is very easy to see within this framework why President Kimball identified the mission of the Church as centering on three main objectives.

1. Preach the gospel in all the world.
2. Redeem the dead of all the earth.
3. Perfect the Saints in all nations.

Through accomplishing these objectives, the Church, under the direction of the priesthood, fulfills the Abrahamic covenant. It is not coincidental that newly ordained nineteen-year-old Melchizedek Priesthood bearers are counseled to fill a mission. On a mission the young men keep their covenant with the Lord with all their time and ability, as do sister missionaries and couples serving missions.

It is also not difficult to see how completely the Savior fulfilled the Abrahamic responsibility of blessing all the world with the gospel, salvation, and life eternal. He fulfilled all with his Atonement, teachings, example, visits to the Nephites and Lost Tribes, and myriad other actions. Mortally speaking, he was in truth a son of Abraham. More than that, Christ had made the original covenant with Abraham; he was its author.

The Lord's Rest

The Book of Mormon offers an additional witness to these truths in Alma the Younger's explanation to the people of Ammonihah of the role of high priests. They were to "teach these things [the saving principles of the gospel] unto the people . . . that thereby the people might know in what manner to look forward to his Son for redemption." Alma stressed that their "calling" was to "teach his commandments unto the children of men, that they also might enter into his rest." (Alma 13:1–2, 6.)

The word *rest* is often seen in conjunction with the priesthood. Abraham wanted "rest" (Abraham 1:2) and sought to administer this blessing of the priesthood to others. The Doctrine and Covenants gives us a distinct definition of rest as it relates to Moses' desire to obtain rest for the children of Israel:

> And this greater priesthood administereth the gospel and holdeth the key of the mysteries of the kingdom, even the key of the knowledge of God.
>
> Therefore, in the ordinances thereof, the power of godliness is manifest. . . .
>
> Now this Moses plainly taught to the children of Israel in the wilderness, and sought diligently to sanctify his people that they might behold the face of God;
>
> But they hardened their hearts and could not endure his presence; therefore, the Lord in his wrath, for his anger was kindled against them, swore that they should not enter into his rest while in the wilderness, *which rest is the fulness of his glory.* (D&C 84:19-20, 23-24, italics added.)

Rest, then, is the fullness of God's glory, and all God's servants have striven to bring their people into its enjoyment. The Melchizedek Priesthood's responsibility, therefore, is to administer the blessings of the gospel to the world that all humanity can enter into the rest of the Lord and enjoy the fullness of his glory.

The emphasis of the priesthood has always been on serving others. To accept the blessings of the priesthood and the gospel and not share them is to deny the very meaning of priesthood authority. It is an act of selfishness and blindness that not only shows a lack of gratitude but also an ignorance of the fundamental truths of the priesthood. The spirit of this responsibility and the charity which should betoken every king of righteousness is eloquently summarized by the Apostle Paul in his letter to the Hebrews: "For every high priest taken from among men is ordained for men in things pertaining to God, that he may offer both gifts and sacrifices for sins: who can have compassion on the ignorant, and on them that are out of the way" (Hebrews 5:1-2).

Of the World or Above the World

If a priesthood holder is to bless the world and thus fulfill the priesthood obligation inherent in the Abrahamic covenant, he must be aware of two attitudes that can hinder how effectively he will influence the world for righteousness: (1) Being of the world or like it, and (2) being above the world or aloof from others not yet part of the covenant. Both attitudes caused major failures among the people recorded in the Old and the New Testaments. They stand in opposition to the very essence of the priesthood, yet they are still pervasive in today's society. We must guard against them.

When God established his covenant people he placed them in the center of the ancient world. Egypt, Babylon, Assyria, Persia, Greece, Rome, and other empires—each came into contact with the people of the covenant. It was the Lord's purpose from the beginning to make Israel a holy and a peculiar people: "Now therefore, if ye will obey my voice indeed, and keep my covenant, then ye shall be a peculiar treasure unto me above all people: for all the earth is mine: and ye shall be unto me a kingdom of priests, and an holy nation" (Exodus 19:5-6). God placed his people in the center of the ancient world, for there they could, if they remained righteous, holy, and peculiar, exert their beneficial influence on and be an example to all the nations of the earth.

Some of the ancient prophets accomplished this objective in large measure. The Old Testament relates the positive influence that Abraham, Joseph, and Moses exerted on Egypt; Daniel and Shadrach, Meshach, and Abed-nego on Babylon and Persia; Jonah on the Assyrians; and Elisha on Naaman. The New Testament follows the same principle with the influence Peter, Paul, and the other disciples had on the Greeks, Romans, and Samaritans.

There is, however, a chance that a peculiar, covenant, and elect people may allow the world's cultures, laws, values, and standards to infiltrate their own. They may become like the world, rather than serving as an example to the world. For example, instead of serving Jehovah in Sinai, the Israelites desired to return to the "fleshpots" of Egypt and their former bondage. Ahab was influenced by Jezebel, Samson was more Philistine than the Philistines, and the people under Samuel wanted to have a king "like all the nations" (1 Samuel 8:5). Throughout the history of Old Testament Israel the children of the covenant embraced the standards and desires of the world.

For this reason the prophets constantly reminded them of their responsibility to choose between being *distinguished from* the world and being *part of* the world. Joshua issued this challenge: "Choose you this day whom ye will serve" (Joshua 24:15). Elijah offered the same choice on Mt. Carmel—"How long halt ye between two opinions? if the Lord be God, follow him: but if Baal, then follow him" (1 Kings 18:21). Obviously, if the Lord's elect become like the world they can no longer fulfill their covenant. This is what Christ meant when he spoke of the salt of the earth losing its savor. "Wherewith shall it [the earth] be salted?" (Matthew 5:13.)

This challenge remains a major stumbling block today. The temptation is ever present to be "like all the nations." Therefore a true king of righteousness will remain peculiar and holy—not aloof—and let his light shine for others to see. The standards and images of the world must never become the ideals of the priesthood bearer or any member of the Church. Alma spoke of the proper priesthood attitude while conversing with the citizens of Ammonihah: "Now they, after being sanctified by the Holy Ghost, having their garments made white, being pure and spotless before God, could not look upon sin save it were with abhorrence; and there were many, exceedingly great many, who were made pure and entered into the rest of the Lord their God" (Alma 13:12). The priesthood bearer must not enter the spacious building of the world but must cling to the rod of iron and eat only from the tree of life. As Lehi did, he will invite others to partake of that fruit also.

The second dangerous attitude is more easily seen in the New Testament. When Christ came, the "elect" had completely turned around their attitude. Instead of embracing the world, they shunned the world, considering themselves superior to it. With this self-righteous attitude, they believed contact with the world rendered one unclean. So strong was their attitude that Nicodemus listened and marvelled as Christ explained to him that, "God so loved the world, that he gave his only begotten Son, that whosoever believeth in him should not perish, but have everlasting life. For God sent not his Son into the world to condemn the world; but that the world through him might be saved." (John 3:16–17, italics added.) Nicodemus and most of the Jews looked for a Messiah who would come as a conquering warrior to put an end to their oppressors. The concept of a Messiah who would die to save all men—Greeks, Romans, and Samaritans included—was foreign to them. He was not coming as a condemning Messiah but as one who saved.

This attitude of remaining separate from the world was evident even among Christ's disciples and Apostles. After the Resurrection and the command to take the gospel to "all the world," it still took the thrice-repeated dream of the unclean animals before Peter understood, after which he preached the gospel to Cornelius. When apprised of his actions, other early Christians were dismayed, saying, "Thou wentest in to men uncircumcised, and didst eat with them" (Acts 11:3). After Peter's careful explanation they concluded with wonder, "Then hath God also to the Gentiles granted repentance unto life" (Acts 11:18). In spite of repeated efforts by Paul and other leaders, apparently the contention concerning the Gentiles continued.

It does not require great insight to understand that a self-righteous attitude will also prevent a priesthood bearer, or a covenant son of Abraham, from blessing the world with happiness, peace, and rest. The priesthood bearer in the Church today must radiate to the world a spirit of love and acceptance in order to bring others to the truths of the gospel. He is to love all people, even when their actions should be condemned. A spirit of pride, superiority, condemnation, or intolerance will prevent righteous priesthood influence as effectively as worldliness. Though priesthood holders cannot "look upon sin save it were with abhorrence" (Alma 13:12), they should nonetheless look on people as the children of Deity and therefore worthy of salvation and love.

Christ, as in all things, is the supreme example of this spirit. The troubled and guilt-ridden sought him out, knowing his attitude toward them was the opposite of that of condemning Pharisees. A true king of righteousness will not let worldliness or self-righteousness stand in the way of blessing "all the families of the earth."

Let us discover some practical methods by which the priesthood covenant regarding "the families of the earth" can be fulfilled. The best place for a priesthood holder to start blessing the world is in his own family, ward, and neighborhood. The major priesthood challenges given to any quorum revolve around nonmembers, part-member families, less-active members, troubled youth, and others with special needs. These are found in every ward and branch of the Church. The scriptures provide an excellent model of an effective way to bless all the families of the earth with the blessings of the gospel, salvation, and eternal life. This model will be discussed in the next chapter.

Wherefore I put thee in remembrance that
thou stir up the gift of God, which is in thee
by the putting on of my hands. For God hath
not given us the spirit of fear; but of power,
and of love, and of a sound mind. Be not
thou therefore ashamed of the testimony of
our Lord, nor of me his prisoner.

—2 Timothy 1:6–8

CHAPTER FIVE

Shepherds Feed the Flocks

Long ago Ezekiel asked a question that causes some reflection. He wrote, "Woe be to the shepherds of Israel that do feed themselves! should not the shepherds feed the flocks?" (Ezekiel 34:2.)

This verse can be applied in many different situations. Who are the shepherds? In the context of the restored Church of Jesus Christ, the shepherds are the Melchizedek Priesthood holders, especially those in positions of authority—but the shepherds can also mean the Church membership in general. All members who are of the seed of Abraham can be considered shepherds. As members of the Church, we often "feed ourselves" through our church attendance, classes, meetings, conferences, and other church activities. This is critical for our spiritual growth, but are we ignoring "the flock"?

Ezekiel follows his question with a description of "the flock": "The *diseased* have ye not strengthened, neither have ye healed that which was *sick*, neither have ye bound up that which was *broken*, neither have ye brought again that which was *driven away*, neither have ye sought that which was *lost*"

(Ezekiel 34:4, italics added). Could the "flock" consist of part-member families, often the result of missionary efforts that yielded a partial harvest? Could the flock consist of less-active families, those who have not been to church in years? Their children do not attend Primary. Their sons will not be made deacons at age twelve or go on missions at age nineteen. Their daughters will not be married in the temple. Their only contact may be an occasional conversation with a home teacher.

Does the flock include nonmember neighbors? Some may be friendly in a casual way, others may be hostile to our religion, while yet others may be longtime friends. Does the flock include the youth—both active and troubled—of our wards?

These four groups of people—part-member families, less-active families, nonmembers, and the youth—are an important part of the responsibilities of a Priesthood Executive Committee, a home teacher, and a stake presidency. Priesthood holders come into almost daily contact with them. Let us apply Ezekiel's description: Are some spiritually diseased, sick, broken, driven away, or lost? How can they be recovered?

We all want to do our duty, to please our Father in Heaven and love his sheep. How do we feed the inactive, the part-member family, the nonmember, the youth, the "one" for whom we were commanded to leave the ninety-nine?

A Simple Answer

There is a simple answer in the Book of Mormon, a step-by-step outline that any priesthood holder, any member, can follow. The answer is so plain that it's a wonder we could read the passages where it is found time and time again without seeing all the truths those passages contain.

We normally read Ammon's missionary experiences with a full-time mission in mind. We focus on his and his brothers' preparation of fasting, prayer, and scripture study. This preparation allowed them to teach "with power and authority of God" (Alma 17:3). However, when we read of Ammon's efforts, at the same time remembering the families in our neighborhoods, we will discover new insights.

The Challenge

Ammon had a great challenge, just as each of us does. The scriptures state this challenge: "For they supposed that great was the work which they had undertaken. And assuredly it was great, for they had undertaken to preach the word of God to a wild and a hardened and a ferocious people." (Alma 17:13-14.) Certainly their challenge was more difficult than most of ours, just as Melchizedek's "neighborhood" posed greater challenges than those most of us face. Many previous efforts had been exerted by the Nephites to bring the Lamanites back into the light, but five hundred years had seen no major successes. Similarly in many wards, bishops, missionaries, home teachers, and youth leaders have tried to convert, reactivate, and lead without meeting major success.

When Ammon and his brothers announce their plans to teach the Lamanites, they are met with skepticism: "Do ye suppose that ye can bring the Lamanites to the knowledge of the truth? Do ye suppose that ye can convince the Lamanites of the incorrectness of the traditions of their fathers, as stiffnecked a people as they are?" (Alma 26:24.) Are our nonmember or inactive neighbors more challenging than this? Do we suppose that we can bring these sons and daughters of God to the knowledge of the truth? The parallels are clear.

Good Examples

What causes Ammon's success? We find a clue in the words of the Lord to the four sons of Mosiah as they set forth on their mission. God counsels them on how to be successful: "And the Lord said unto them also: Go forth among the Lamanites, thy brethren, and establish my word; yet ye shall be patient in long-suffering and afflictions, that ye may show forth good examples unto them in me, and I will make an instrument of thee in my hands unto the salvation of many souls" (Alma 17:11).

The Lord tells them that setting a "good example" will be the key. We've heard that before. Sometimes we allow it to be a rationalization for nonactivity in spreading the gospel message.

We will set a good example for our neighbors, we think, by living our religion, and eventually they will knock on our doors and ask us why our lives are so different. Then we'll explain the truths of the Church and they will believe. We'll just go about our business knowing they are watching. There is truth in this, and yet we sense there is more to do than that.

I Will Be Thy Servant

Reading on in Alma 17:25 we discover in the words of Ammon to King Lamoni the specific example the Lord would counsel us to set: "I will be thy servant" (Alma 17:25). Ammon does not enter the land of Ishmael and immediately begin preaching. He has to lay the foundation first. He has to be a good example, and that means giving service. His conversation with the king is gracious and sincere. The scriptures indicate that "Lamoni was much pleased with Ammon" (Alma 17:24). Who wouldn't be impressed with a young Nephite, the son of a king, who had given up his rights to a kingdom to be a Lamanite servant. The example the Lord would have us set is one of service to our neighbors, not just going about our business living the gospel, feeding ourselves, and hoping others will see and decide to follow.

Lamoni sets Ammon over his flocks. Perhaps this is a test of Ammon's loyalty. Both know what is done to servants who lose sheep—they forfeit their life. Lamoni has an interesting value system: a man's life is worth less than that of a sheep. Perhaps Lamoni wants to see the sincerity and depth of Ammon's desire to serve, just as our own neighbors might test the strength of our commitment to serve. Does our service spring from a sense of religious duty or from sincere love and caring?

Lead Them to Believe

The opportunity soon comes for Ammon to prove his commitment to Lamoni and his fellow servants. The scattering of Lamoni's flocks is attempted almost immediately. Some might have seen this as a disaster, a time to withdraw, but Ammon sees it as a blessing. He sees the fear and weeping of his fellow servants and says in his heart, "I will show forth my power unto these my fellow-servants . . . in restoring these flocks unto the king, that I may *win the hearts of these my fellow-servants,* that I may *lead them to believe* in my words" (Alma 17:29, italics added). What a marvelous truth Ammon expresses! The winning of a man's heart leads him to believe. Let us think of our neighbors in light of this verse. Have we won their hearts? It is our responsibility to lead them to believe in the words of eternal life. Perhaps we have thought in the past it was their responsibility primarily to believe and accept.

Ammon has not yet said a word about religion, but he has been busy laying the groundwork; he has been winning hearts. The pieces all fit:

1. "Good examples."
2. "I will be thy servant."
3. "I may win the hearts . . . that I may lead them to believe."

A good example of service wins hearts and prepares the way for belief. It leads people to believe. It is in reality very simple.

His Brethren

From verse 30 we can learn another key: "And now, these were the thoughts of Ammon, when he saw the afflictions of those whom *he termed to be his brethren*" (Alma 17:30, italics added). The attitude reflected in these words is that Ammon, a king's son, truly views Lamanite slaves, whose lives are valued less than a sheep's, as his brethren. He does not feel superior to them, nor does he condemn them for their base "traditions." He does not believe God loves him more than them, or that he is more precious in the sight of God and Christ than they are. He does not show them intolerance and prejudice because they are different. They are his brethren. We can reasonably assume that they feel his acceptance of them as brothers.

Do we project the same attitude to our neighbors, or do they view us as cliquish, intolerant, and condemnatory. One of the greatest attributes of Christ was his ability to draw the spiritually sick to him through the power of his love and acceptance of them. There was never any doubt about how he felt about their sins, nor was there doubt of his total commitment and love of the person. He was ready to help them if they would allow him to. Do our neighbors feel we condemn or judge them, or have we radiated to them our love and fellowship in a sincere manner?

He Is a Friend

As the story proceeds, Ammon defends the flocks and saves his fellow servants. He then returns to the king's home and prepares the king's horses for an upcoming journey. In other words, he is still serving. The Lamanite servants return to the king to tell him of Ammon's miraculous defense of the king's flocks. When Lamoni hears of all that Ammon has done, he concludes, "Surely this is more than a man." He wonders if Ammon is not the "Great Spirit." In the servants' answer to the king we learn of another key to Ammon's success: "Whether he be the Great Spirit or a man, we know not; but this much we do know . . . , *we know that he is a friend to the king*" (Alma 18:3, italics added). How marvelous this is that the servants of the king would bear witness to Lamoni of Ammon's friendship! What power for good there would be if one of our nonmember neighbors said to another, "I don't know much about my Mormon neighbors or about their religion, but one thing I do know, they are your friends and my friends." What power there would be for good if the rebellious Aaronic priesthood boy, or the less-active family, knew and testified to each other about the solid friendship they felt from us and our families!

The Stirrings of Conscience

Something strange and wonderful begins to happen to Lamoni at this point. He obviously has some misconceptions about Ammon's identity. The Lord steps into Lamoni's life and begins to stir his conscience. The scriptures tell us of these stirrings in the following verse: "Notwithstanding they believed in a Great Spirit, they supposed that whatsoever they did was right; nevertheless, Lamoni began to fear exceedingly, with fear lest he had done wrong in slaying his servants'' (Alma 18:5). Lamoni is being prepared by the Spirit to hear the words of life and salvation. In his value system he had not thought it was wrong to slay his servants. Now, confronted with Ammon's example of friendship and service, he begins to reevaluate his life.

Often our neighbors see nothing wrong in their lifestyles, or, if they do, need encouragement to change. The nonmember may see nothing wrong in drinking alcohol. The husband or wife of a part-member family may not value church attendance, baptism, or a deeper closeness with the spouse. The less active may not see a need for a temple marriage, the payment of tithes, or the ordination of their sons. The rebellious priest perhaps sees nothing wrong in cigarettes, hard rock music, or rejecting a mission call. Could it be possible that an example of service and friendship could stir their consciences and cause a reevaluation? Let us look at our growing list of key statements:

1. "Good examples."
2. "I will be thy servant."
3. "I may win the hearts . . . that I may lead them to believe."
4. "We know that he is a friend."
5. "Nevertheless, Lamoni began to fear exceedingly, with fear lest he had done wrong" (the stirrings of conscience).

The Most Faithful Servant

Lamoni asks his servants where Ammon is. When he is told that Ammon is preparing his horses and chariots for the king's approaching journey, he is more astonished "because of the faithfulness of Ammon." Ammon is still serving. In Lamoni's words we find the next key in Ammon's process of preparing him to hear the gospel. "Surely there has not been any servant among all my servants that has been so faithful as this man" (Alma 18:10). Not only is Ammon the king's servant and friend, he is also the greatest of each the king has ever had. What could happen if our neighbors felt that of all their neighbors and friends, they had never had any as true and faithful as ourselves? What could happen if the less-active family felt that they had the most faithful home teacher they had ever had? In all points Ammon is magnifying his priesthood calling and fulfilling the Abrahamic covenant.

"I Durst Not"

The next point in Ammon's relationship with Lamoni is an interesting one. Lamoni says, "I would desire him that he come in unto me, but I durst not" (Alma 18:11). Lamoni wants to speak with Ammon, but he is afraid. Ammon enters the room at about this time and is told by another servant that the king desires to speak with him. Ammon asks the king, "What wilt thou that I should do for thee, O king?" Lamoni doesn't answer "for he knew not what he should say unto him." (Alma 18:14.) There then follows "an hour" of silence. How curious! Ammon's heart is burning to tell the king all the wonders and joys of the gospel and the king is desirous to hear them and understand Ammon, but they stand in silence. Have we ever perceived that our neighbors might want to talk of the deep things of their heart, but are afraid? Do we feel that the fear to speak of religion is one-sided?

The Thoughts of My Heart

Ammon, receiving knowledge from the Spirit to perceive "the thoughts of the king," speaks first (Alma 18:16). He breaks the ice, and Lamoni opens to Ammon the thoughts of his heart. In doing so he gives us the last key to Ammon's success, the one we all want and sometimes use without first laying the proper foundation. Lamoni, perceiving the discernment of Ammon, asks him, "How knowest thou the thoughts of my heart? Thou mayest speak boldly, and tell me concerning these things." (Alma 18:20.) Perhaps the greatest result of friendship and service is knowing the thoughts of another's heart. Isn't this a good definition of friendship and brotherhood? Don't we want others to understand us and perceive the thoughts, needs, and desires of our hearts and minds?

Speak with Boldness

All that Ammon "desires" is that Lamoni will "hearken unto [his] words." Lamoni answers, "I will believe all thy words." Ammon then "began to speak unto him *with boldness*." (Alma 18:22–24.) We have often been told by our leaders to speak with boldness. Now we understand that appropriate preparation allows us to do so with effectiveness.

We all know the result of Ammon's simple teaching of the gospel. Lamoni was what some members and missionaries would call a "golden contact," but it was Ammon's example that made Lamoni golden; he did not start out that way. Neither will most of our neighbors. We must *lead* them to the point of goldenness. In doing so we become the true seed of Abraham.

The Greatness of Ammon

The story of Ammon and his brothers continues, adding testimony of the power of our key statements, which are:

1. "Good examples."
2. "I will be thy servant."
3. "I may win the hearts of these my fellow servants that I may lead them to believe in my words."
4. "We know that he is a friend."
5. Lamoni began to "fear exceedingly, with fear lest he had done wrong" (the stirrings of conscience).
6. "Surely there has not been any servant among all of my servants that has been so faithful as this man."
7. "I would desire him that he come in unto me, but I durst not."
8. "He knew not what he should say unto him."
9. "How knowest thou the thoughts of my heart?"
10. "Thou mayest speak boldly."
11. "I will believe all thy words."

Ammon's confrontation with Lamoni's antagonistic father is added proof that Ammon truly magnified his calling to preach the gospel. Perhaps there is no better example of the problems inherent in a part-member family than the account recorded in Alma 20. The old king's hatred of Nephites is changed by Ammon's love and friendship: "He saw that Ammon had no desire to destroy him, and *when also he saw the great love* he had for his son Lamoni, he was astonished exceedingly, and said . . . , I shall greatly desire to see thee" (Alma 20:26–27, italics added). Love and example turn the key for Lamoni's angry father. When Aaron and his fellow missionaries reach the home of Lamoni's father, offering themselves as servants, he tells them, "I have been somewhat troubled in mind because of the generosity and the greatness of the words of thy brother Ammon" (Alma 22:3). Once again "good examples" have opened doors. Lamoni's father ties the success of Ammon's labors to his perception of "the great love" of Ammon for Lamoni. As Melchizedek Priesthood bearers, we would do well to adopt Ammon's spirit of love and his view of the importance of the gospel.

There is one more essential key that adds to those already given; this key is the attitude of deep love that the four sons of Mosiah and their companions cultivate before and during their missions. This love is the taproot that nourishes all the other principles. It is the most essential attitude that priesthood bearers must exhibit to successfully magnify their callings. Without it priesthood holders will never be effective. It is the engine that turns the gospel of Christ and motivates the true son of Abraham. It is the key to fulfilling the great Abrahamic promise that all nations would be blessed. It represents the greatness of Ammon.

The attitude of the sons of Mosiah is described in the following manner: "Now they were desirous that salvation should be declared to every creature, *for they could not bear that any human soul should perish;* yea, even the very thoughts that any soul should endure endless torment did cause them to quake and tremble" (Mosiah 28:3, italics added). When we as priesthood bearers and members of the Church "cannot bear that any human soul" should be without the blessings of the gospel, we will not need exhortation or prodding to work with nonmembers, part-members, less-active members, or rebellious youth.

Our "good example" will come naturally. It is not always easy to befriend the other sheep of the fold, but they need to be fed from the Savior's pure pastures. It does not need to take years and years for them to feel genuine love from those of us who have already pastured in the Savior's abundant meadows of life.

I remember listening to my mother read to me as a boy the story of Ammon defending the flocks at the waters of Sebus. I would look at the picture and imagine Ammon's great strength. He was a hero, a mighty man. I thought his greatness arose from his ability to use a sling and a sword. I loved the story, but I have since come to realize that Ammon was great because he fit perfectly the definition of greatness given by the Master Shepherd, "He that is greatest among you shall be your servant" (Matthew 23:11). Ammon has taught us all the definition of greatness. His greatness rested in the humility and service with which he fed the flocks of the Shepherd whose example he followed. He was a true son of Abraham.

A certain nobleman had a spot of land, very
choice; and he said unto his servants: Go ye
unto my vineyard, even upon this very choice
piece of land, and plant twelve olive-trees;
and set watchmen round about them, and
build a tower, that one may overlook the land
round about, to be a watchman upon the
tower, that mine olive-trees may not be
broken down when the enemy shall come to
spoil and take upon themselves the fruit of
my vineyard.

−D&C 101:44−45

CHAPTER SIX

"Magnify Thine Office"

Perhaps the most commonly used expression relative to the
priesthood is "magnify thy calling." The preceding chapters
have given some ideas on how a man magnifies his callings in
the priesthood. This involves his family, the Church, and the
world, and his responsibility to bless them with peace and rest.
Let us now study a definition of *magnify* given in the Book of
Mormon and apply that definition to the various responsibilities
of the priesthood.

In the first chapter of Jacob, we read that the Nephites
"began to grow hard in their hearts, and indulge themselves
somewhat in wicked practices" (Jacob 1:15). There were three
basic attitudes or desires about which Jacob was concerned: (1)
His people were seeking material wealth and riches and were
allowing their possessions to fill them with pride. (2) Some were
using the scriptures to justify lustful desires. (3) They despised
and hated the Lamanites because of their dark skins and cultural "filthiness."

After identifying these major concerns, Jacob gathered the
people together "in the temple, having first obtained [his] er-

rand from the Lord." Jacob and his brother Joseph "had been consecrated priests and teachers of the people, by the hand of Nephi." They took their ordination seriously. Jacob's attitude to his calling is reflected in the following statement which defines the word *magnify*: "And we did magnify our office unto the Lord, taking upon us the responsibility, answering the sins of the people upon our own heads if we did not teach them the word of God with all diligence; wherefore, by laboring with our might their blood might not come upon our garments; otherwise their blood would come upon our garments, and we would not be found spotless at the last day" (Jacob 1:17–19).

As a consecrated priest and teacher, Jacob felt a responsibility for those he served. Magnifying a priesthood calling implies recognizing that responsibility. "Having first obtained [his] errand from the Lord," Jacob knew he had to teach his people, seeking the approbation of the Spirit in all that he would teach and exhort.

Magnifying a priesthood calling consists partly of teaching others "with all diligence" the consequences of their sins and attitudes. Failure to do so brings the priesthood bearer under condemnation. He receives "the sins of the people upon [his] own head." This is what it means to magnify a calling. One must teach that people can avoid transgression, and that when transgression has been committed there is a loving pathway that leads to repentance.

There is ample scriptural support for this interpretation. When Ezekiel was issued a call to be a "watchman" over Israel, the Lord instructed him in his responsibility. He appropriately used the analogy of war to stress his point, for, in a way, we are all engaged in a war—the war for the souls of men. "But if the watchman see the sword come," the Lord explained, "and blow not the trumpet, and the people be not warned; if the sword come, and take any person from among them, he is taken away in his iniquity; but his blood will I require at the watchman's hand." The Lord then applied this principle to Ezekiel's priesthood calling.

> So thou, O son of man, I have set thee a watchman unto the house of Israel; therefore thou shalt hear the word at my mouth, and warn them from me.

When I say unto the wicked, O wicked man, thou shalt surely die; if thou dost not speak to warn the wicked from his way, that wicked man shall die in his iniquity; but his blood will I require at thine hand.

Nevertheless, if thou warn the wicked of his way to turn from it; if he do not turn from his way, he shall die in his iniquity; but thou hast delivered thy soul. (Ezekiel 33:6–9.)

The Lord is very straightforward in these verses. Those who have turned from the straight and narrow path must hear "the trumpet" of the watchman. They must be taught "with all diligence." This is the responsibility of the priesthood bearers, for they are set as watchmen over the Church.

This function of the priesthood is so basic that it is included in the instructions to the Aaronic Priesthood given at the organization of the Restored Church in the last days: "The teacher's duty is to watch over the church always, and be with and strengthen them," the Lord told Joseph Smith. "And see that there is no iniquity in the church, neither hardness with each other, neither lying, backbiting, nor evil speaking; and see that the church meet together often, and also see that all the members do their duty." (D&C 20:53–55.)

The Old Testament gives an excellent example of this principle in practice. In the early chapters of 1 Samuel we are introduced to the high priest Eli. His two sons Hophni and Phineas are described as "sons of Belial; they knew not the Lord" (1 Samuel 2:12). They are, however, priests serving in the ordinances of the law of Moses. Their evil ways turn people from proper worship, causing them to abhor "the offering of the Lord"; therefore "the sin of the young men was very great" (1 Samuel 2:17).

Eli's responsibility, both as a father and as the high priest, is to correct the actions of his sons. He mildly chastises his sons by saying, "It is no good report that I hear: ye make the Lord's people to transgress" (1 Samuel 2:24). Although the young men refuse to listen, Eli does nothing. At this time the child Samuel is called to be the Lord's prophet and messenger. He is instructed to give to Eli the following message: "For I have told him that I will judge his house for ever for the iniquity which he knoweth;

because his sons made themselves vile, and he restrained them not" (1 Samuel 3:13). Though Samuel "feared to shew Eli the vision," he "told him every whit, and hid nothing from him" (1 Samuel 3:15, 18). As a "watchman," Eli failed to restrain his sons. By contrast, Samuel hid nothing. Both serve as excellent examples of the magnification of which Jacob spoke.

As is seen in Samuel's hesitation, it is not always easy to warn another of transgression or of the attitudes that will lead to it. In the Book of Mormon Jacob approached his task with great reluctance. "It grieveth my soul and causeth me to shrink with shame before the presence of my Maker, that I must testify unto you concerning the wickedness of your hearts," he told his people. He then explained why his task was so difficult. "And also it grieveth me that I must use so much boldness of speech concerning you, before your wives and your children. . . . But, notwithstanding the greatness of the task, I must do according to the strict commands of God, and tell you concerning your wickedness and abominations, in the presence of the pure in heart. . . . I must tell you the truth according to the plainness of the word of God." (Jacob 2:6–7, 10–11.)

This reluctance and anxiety often stands in the way of a priesthood holder's ability to magnify his calling. Nobody enjoys issuing warnings. Jacob didn't. Samuel didn't. Our General Authorities today don't, nor do bishops, quorum leaders, or home teachers. But they "take upon [themselves] the responsibility" because they are the "watchmen."

Let's ask ourselves some questions in order to examine the practicality of these principles. What is the responsibility of a bishop when he perceives attitudes, desires, or behaviors in his ward that will cause the members to stray from the paths of righteousness? What responsibility does he carry towards those who break the Word of Wisdom, do not pay tithing, slip into immoral behavior, or abuse their families? What is the responsibility of an elders quorum president to the prospective elders he serves or to the elders who fail to home teach? What is the responsibility of a home teacher to a family who is inactive or fails to live the principles that lead to happiness? What is the responsibility of a father to a teenage son whose acceptance of the world's standards is leading him deeper and deeper into temptation and probable sin. The answer to all of these questions is that the priesthood leader must be a faithful watchman and give the proper warning.

In each of these cases and dozens more it is difficult to fill the position of watchman, but the Lord is specific. Those who fail to "magnify [their] office" "answer the sins of the people upon [their] own heads."

There is a proper way to magnify one's calling. One does not warn with self-righteousness, railing, browbeating, or condemnatory cries of repentance. One must sound the trumpet with love, charity, understanding, invitation, and acceptance of the individual. To do otherwise is to drive the sheep further into the wilderness. Jacob fulfilled his responsibility with firmness coupled with love and sincere anxiety. The warning voice of invitation is portrayed most beautifully by the Savior. There is never any doubt about his attitude towards disobedience and sin, and there is also never any doubt concerning his love for the sinner.

In section 50 of the Doctrine and Covenants the Lord plainly states how we should not warn others: "Not with railing accusation, that ye be not overcome, neither with boasting nor rejoicing, lest you be seized therewith" (D&C 50:33). Railing, boasting, or rejoicing in another's transgressions are attitudes foreign to a true son of Abraham. Meekness, charity, and patience belong to the priesthood. Paul's definition of charity is appropriate to remember: "Charity suffereth long, and is kind; charity envieth not; charity vaunteth not itself, is not puffed up. Doth not behave itself unseemly, seeketh not her own, is not easily provoked, thinketh no evil; rejoiceth not in iniquity, but rejoiceth in the truth; beareth all things, believeth all things, hopeth all things, endureth all things." (1 Corinthians 13:4-7.)

Even if the time comes when a sharp or strong reproof is needed, the attitude of love must be present and controlled by the Holy Spirit. Indeed, the Lord counsels us to show "forth afterwards an increase of love toward him whom thou hast reproved, lest he esteem thee to be his enemy; that he may know that thy faithfulness is stronger than the cords of death" (D&C 121:43-44).

A sharp reproof does not mean an angry one, but that is often how we interpret the term. Just prior to his death, Lehi explained to Laman and Lemuel the correct interpretation. Nephi, he said, "hath sought . . . your own eternal welfare. . . . Ye say that he hath used sharpness; ye say that he hath been angry with you; but behold, his sharpness was the sharpness of the power of the word of God, which was in him; and that which ye call anger was the truth. . . ." (2 Nephi 1:25-26.)

To "reprove betimes with sharpness" (D&C 121:43), then, means to correct with the truth under the influence of the Spirit while motivated by a desire for the eternal welfare of the person one is reproving. A sharp reproof should be followed by an "increase" of love. That increased love witnesses to the rebuked one that the warning was made out of concern for his eternal salvation and not as a condemning accusation.

Fulfilling this priesthood responsibility is not easy, but it is necessary. When done with charity and under the guidance of the Spirit, it constitutes one of the major ways that a son of Abraham brings to his fellowmen the happiness, peace, and rest of the gospel.

The power and authority of the higher, or
Melchizedek Priesthood, is to hold the keys of
all the spiritual blessings of the church – to
have the privilege of receiving the mysteries
of the kingdom of heaven, to have the heavens opened unto them, to commune with the
general assembly and church of the Firstborn,
and to enjoy the communion and presence of
God the Father, and Jesus the mediator of
the new covenant.

–D&C 107:18–19

CHAPTER SEVEN

Releasing Priesthood Power

We have seen that the major thrust of the priesthood is minister-
ing the blessings of the gospel to others. We have also outlined a
model showing an effective way to invite others to enjoy the
blessings of the gospel. Now we will seek an understanding of
the principles that govern the release of priesthood power.

The Will of God

There appear to be two very basic truths that provide the
foundation upon which priesthood power rests. The first pillar
of power is made available to priesthood bearers as they bring
themselves in line with the will of God. The second is dependent
on their personal purity and their willingness to submit to the
cleansing power of the Savior. When true sons of Abraham
stand before the Lord in purity and desire to do his will, they
can exercise great power.

The scriptures record numerous experiences of past patriarchs who controlled the elements in behalf of their people. The

Joseph Smith Translation of Genesis 14 gives an extensive list of
what the priesthood can accomplish:

> For God having sworn unto Enoch and unto his seed
> with an oath by himself; that every one being ordained
> after this order and calling should have power, by faith, to
> break mountains, to divide the seas, to dry up waters, to
> turn them out of their course;
>
> To put at defiance the armies of nations, to divide the
> earth, to break every band, to stand in the presence of
> God; *to do all things according to his will, according to
> his command,* subdue principalities and powers; and *this
> by the will of the Son of God* which was from before the
> foundation of the world (JST, Genesis 14:30–31, italics add-
> ed).

All these blessings, the outward manifestations of power, and
the spiritual manifestation of intelligence are contingent on the
will of God. In the verses quoted above, the Lord plainly states
that priesthood bearers can "do all things according to his will,
according to his command."

Before the priesthood can be manifested, a true king of righteousness must know that the will of the Lord is being done and
that he, the priesthood holder, has been either commanded to
perform or pronounce the blessing or justified in his decision to
do so. This principle is taught plainly throughout the scriptures,
and implies a oneness with God. Christ taught the principle to
the Apostles at the Last Supper, comparing himself to a vine and
the Apostles to branches:

> Abide in me, and I in you. As the branch cannot bear
> fruit of itself, except it abide in the vine; no more can ye,
> except ye abide in me.
>
> I am the vine, ye are the branches: He that abideth in
> me, and I in him, the same bringeth forth much fruit: for
> without me ye can do nothing.
>
> If ye abide in me, and my words abide in you, ye shall
> ask what ye will, and it shall be done unto you. (John
> 15:4–5, 7.)

The Book of Mormon contains the story of Nephi the son of Helaman, to whom God gave the type of power spoken of in Genesis 14. After returning from extensive missions and boldly standing before the corrupt judges of Zarahemla, Nephi was commanded to go throughout the land again and preach repentance to his people. The Lord then gave Nephi a wonderful promise:

> Blessed art thou, Nephi, for those things which thou hast done; for I have beheld how thou hast with unwearyingness declared the word, which I have given unto thee, unto this people. And thou hast not feared them, and hast not sought thine own life, but hast sought my will, and to keep my commandments.
>
> And now, because thou hast done this with such unwearyingness, behold, I will bless thee forever; and I will make thee mighty in word and in deed, in faith and in works; yea, even that *all things shall be done unto thee according to thy word, for thou shalt not ask that which is contrary to my will.*
>
> Behold, thou art Nephi, and I am God. Behold, I declare it unto thee in the presence of mine angels, that ye shall have power over this people, and shall smite the earth with famine, and with pestilence, and destruction, according to the wickedness of this people.
>
> Behold, I give unto you power, that whatsoever ye shall seal on earth shall be sealed in heaven; and whatsoever ye shall loose on earth shall be loosed in heaven; and thus shall ye have power among this people. (Helaman 10:4–7, italics added.)

The important element in this passage is the explanation of why God could give Nephi such extensive power. He knew Nephi would not do anything contrary to his will. Because Nephi's heart and mind were one with God, God could make his power one with Nephi.

Every priesthood holder should seek to establish this oneness with the Godhead. Christ constantly invited his disciples and Apostles to be one with him as he was with his Father. This is beautifully expressed in the great Intercessory Prayer in John 17. The fullest exercise of the priesthood is maintained by this oneness. To magnify the priesthood, a king of righteousness will seek this oneness; for only with this unity can he minister the blessings of the priesthood in a way acceptable to the Lord.

The Holy Ghost is a key factor in this principle, for it is through the Holy Ghost that a man knows the will of the Father and can therefore pronounce blessings with confidence. A priesthood holder must therefore cultivate the Spirit in his own life in order to have a clear channel to the will of the Father.

Paul referred to Christ as the great high priest "after the order of Melchizedec" (Hebrews 5:6). It should not surprise us, therefore, to discover that the Savior provides the ultimate and perfect example of this principle. Notice the total unity of Christ's will with that of the Father as expressed in the following verse: "I can of mine own self do nothing: as I hear, I judge: and my judgment is just; because I seek not mine own will, but the will of the Father which hath sent me" (John 5:30). Christ's judgment and use of power was always just because he constantly did the will of the Father. This principle is repeated many times in the life and statements of the Savior.

An examination of a few additional examples can help us realize the need of this same unity in our own use of priesthood authority. Speaking of his "doctrine," Christ stated, "My doctrine is not mine, but his that sent me" (John 7:16). In the eighth chapter of John, Jesus proclaimed, "I do nothing of myself" (John 8:28). Jesus knew that the Father was always with him because of the Son's commitment to "do always those things that please him" (John 8:29). Prior to the atoning week of sacrifice Jesus told the Jews: "For I have not spoken of myself; but the Father which sent me, he gave me a commandment, what I should say, and what I should speak" (John 12:49).

During the Last Supper Jesus assured his Apostles again that he shared a oneness with the Father. To Philip's desire to see the Father, Jesus replied, "Believest thou not that I am in the Father, and the Father in me? the words that I speak unto you I speak not of myself: but the Father that dwelleth in me, he doeth the works." (John 14:10.)

Could we find a better example of the proper use of authority anywhere in scripture than that of the Savior himself? If Christ did nothing without being in total accord with the Father's will, should we pronounce blessings, give promises, perform ordinances, or expound doctrine without also making sure through the power of the Holy Ghost that our words and works are in line with the Father's will?

There are times when, for various reasons, we are not confident that we know the will of the Lord. Probably all priesthood bearers have had this experience. When we have prayed or fasted and sought the Spirit to the best of our ability and we do not feel we know the Lord's will, blessings can still be bestowed. We should not presume to pronounce on another's head promises which have not been directed by the still, small voice; rather, let our words be a humble request that the Lord will hear our prayers and bestow desired blessings in accordance with his will. The parables of the unjust judge and the widow (Luke 18) and of the importuning friend (Luke 11) teach the power of a continual request for help and inspiration.

Purified and Cleansed

The second mighty truth necessary for releasing priesthood power for the benefit of others is that of being purified and cleansed. A powerful scripture found in Doctrine and Covenants 50 gives further light:

> He that is ordained of God and sent forth, the same is appointed to be the greatest, notwithstanding he is the least and the servant of all.
>
> Wherefore, he is possessor of all things; for all things are subject unto him, both in heaven and on the earth, the life and the light, the Spirit and the power, sent forth by the will of the Father through Jesus Christ, his Son.
>
> But no man is possessor of all things except he be purified and cleansed from all sin.
>
> And if ye are purified and cleansed from all sin, ye shall ask whatsoever you will in the name of Jesus and it shall be done.
>
> But know this, it shall be given you what you shall ask; and as ye are appointed to the head, the spirits shall be subject unto you. (D&C 50:26–30.)

Once again we read of power given to those who are "ordained of God." They are going forth to serve, which is consistent with what we have discussed in earlier chapters. All things become subject to such a servant, dependent upon his personal worthiness. He must strive to be purified from all sin if he is to enjoy such a blessing.

This purification comes through the atonement of Jesus Christ and the cleansing fire of the Holy Ghost. It is maintained by (1) constant humility, (2) prayer, and (3) steadfastness in the faith of Christ. King Benjamin stresses retaining a remission of sins and purity by these three qualities (see Mosiah 4:11–12).

We can conclude that personal purity or righteousness, therefore, is the second principle upon which priesthood power rests. It is also the key to understanding the will of God through the Holy Ghost. Doctrine and Covenants 50:30 promises that "it shall be given you what you shall ask," thus enabling the individual to have the oneness with Deity that is required. These are simple and plain principles.

It is consistent with the character of the Godhead that their authority can be maintained among mortals only by the personal purity of righteous priesthood bearers and by means of a shared oneness with divine will. As in all things Christ is the perfect example. His personal purity cannot be denied, for he had no sin. Throughout the Gospels he stresses constantly that he came "to do the will of [his] Father." "I do nothing of myself," he taught his Jewish critics, "but as my Father hath taught me, I speak these things. And he that sent me is with me: the Father hath not left me alone; for I do always those things that please him." (John 8:28–29.) Is it any wonder that Christ performed such miracles of healing and power or that he could bestow such spiritual blessings and revelation upon his followers?

The principle of personal righteousness and purity is often taught in the scriptures in conjunction with receiving the priesthood. An examination of two other verses will serve as second witnesses to these truths. We have already referred to Alma 13, but another look at this chapter reveals more truth:

> Now, as I said concerning the holy order, or this high priesthood, there were many who were ordained and became high priests of God; and it was on account of their

exceeding faith and repentance, *and their righteousness before God,* they choosing to repent and work righteousness rather than to perish;

Therefore they were called after this holy order, and were *sanctified,* and *their garments were washed white through the blood of the Lamb.*

Now they, after being *sanctified by the Holy Ghost,* having their garments made white, being pure and spotless before God, could not look upon sin save it were with abhorrence; and there were many, exceedingly great many, *who were made pure* and entered into the rest of the Lord their God.

And now, my brethren, I would that ye should *humble yourselves* before God, and bring forth fruit meet for repentance, that ye may also enter into that rest. (Alma 13:10–13, italics added.)

Faith, repentance, righteousness, sanctification by the Holy Ghost, and purity are all spoken of by Alma in his description of those who received the holy order of the Melchizedek Priesthood. In this verse, the very appearance of sin is abhorrent to the sanctified. Through these righteous attributes priests became qualified to enter God's rest and become one with him.

Doctrine and Covenants 121 bears another strong witness to the importance of personal righteousness. We examined this chapter closely in discussing the role of a patriarch to his family. In this revelation the Lord states "that the rights of the priesthood are inseparably connected with the powers of heaven, and that the powers of heaven cannot be controlled nor handled only upon the principles of righteousness" (D&C 121:36). This verse is followed by the Lord's explanation of what happens when the priesthood is handled upon other principles. "When we undertake to cover our sins, or to gratify our pride, our vain ambition, or to exercise control or dominion or compulsion upon the souls of the children of men, in any degree of unrighteousness, behold, the heavens withdraw themselves; the Spirit of the Lord is grieved; and when it is withdrawn, Amen to the priesthood or the authority of that man" (D&C 121:36–37). This is a strong statement. Priesthood can be conferred on men, but when that priesthood is used any other way than by righteousness, the

Lord declares "Amen" to the man's priesthood authority. Not only is righteousness required but also without it there is no priesthood authority.

Three Keys

From our review of the principles we just discussed, we can conclude that before a Melchizedek Priesthood bearer attempts to use his authority he would do well to ask himself three basic questions:

1. Am I exercising my authority for the benefit of others? Am I seeking their happiness, peace, and rest?
2. Have I sought the will of the Lord and do I know through the Holy Ghost what that will is?
3. Am I personally worthy to exercise the priesthood? Am I pure and righteous?

If these three requirements are filled, the power of the priesthood can be manifested with perfect confidence. This in large measure is what the Lord means when he concludes Doctrine and Covenants 121 with this promise: "Let thy bowels also be full of charity towards all men, and to the household of faith, and let virtue garnish thy thoughts unceasingly; *then shall thy confidence wax strong in the presence of God;* and the doctrine of the priesthood shall distil upon thy soul as the dews from heaven" (D&C 121:45, italics added).

Faith and the Priesthood

In our discussion on priesthood power we have not spoken of faith; however, it is impossible to separate the two. Let us, therefore, attempt to place faith in a proper context with the above principles. The last verse quoted (D&C 121:45) is an excellent description of faith and priesthood. When our confidence waxes strong we have faith. Our confidence is not only faith in God's ability to perform miracles and blessings, but a personal confidence of individual worthiness that comes from righteousness, charity, and virtuous thought.

Joseph Smith teaches in the *Lectures on Faith* that faith is a power: "We understand that when a man works by faith he works by mental exertion instead of physical force. It is by words instead of exerting his physical powers, with which every being works when he works by faith." (*Lectures on Faith*, 7:3.) The same lecture provides the key to obtaining faith. This important teaching gives a clear understanding of the meaning of "confidence" in the presence of God. Once this key to faith is understood, the power of faith as it relates to the priesthood is unlocked.

Joseph Smith taught that faith rests on three main pillars. First, one must have "the idea that [God] actually exists." This knowledge, Joseph Smith demonstrates, comes from the testimony of the "fathers," as we discussed in an earlier chapter. Second, one must have a "correct idea of his character, perfections and attributes." These are supplied through the testimonies recorded in the scriptures. Third, one must have "an actual knowledge that the course of life which he is pursuing is according to [God's] will." (*Lectures on Faith*, 3:3–5.) This third pillar is crucial, but how can we know our life is in accordance with God's will? Obviously, righteousness, purity, and obedience are required to gain such an assurance. Individual faith rests on a solid foundation of individual righteousness. Thus we see another witness to the earlier teachings on purity.

As a man perfects his life, he gains perfect faith or confidence in God to use the priesthood, and with this perfecting process the ability to use the priesthood to benefit others increases. A king of righteousness will have a deep desire to put his life completely in accordance with God's will in order to acquire and maintain a faith capable of blessing others with the powers of the priesthood. This is likely one reason why Abraham desired to receive instructions and to obey commandments.

The Sacrifice of All Earthly Things

In the sixth lecture on faith Joseph Smith gave further instruction on how to obtain the knowledge that our lives are in accordance with God's will:

Let us here observe, that a religion that does not require the sacrifice of all things never has power sufficient
to produce the faith necessary unto life and salvation; for,
from the first existence of man, the faith necessary unto
the enjoyment of life and salvation never could be obtained
without the sacrifice of all earthly things. It was through
this sacrifice, and this only, that God has ordained that
men should enjoy eternal life; and it is through the medi-
um of the sacrifice of all earthly things that men do actually know that they are doing the things that are well
pleasing in the sight of God. (*Lectures on Faith,* 6:7.)

These truths apply to anyone who desires faith sufficient to
win salvation, but they are particularly useful to the priesthood
bearer, for he must have faith to perform its functions. The sacrifice of earthly or worldly things produces and sustains faith.
Joseph Smith further teaches that this sacrifice produces "unshaken confidence":

But those who have not made this sacrifice to God do
not know that the course which they pursue is well pleasing in his sight; for whatever may be their belief or their
opinion, it is a matter of doubt and uncertainty in their
mind; and where doubt and uncertainty are there faith is
not, nor can it be. *For doubt and faith do not exist in the
same person at the same time*; so that persons whose
minds are under doubts and fears cannot have unshaken
confidence; and where unshaken confidence is not there
faith is weak. (*Lectures on Faith,* 6:12, italics added.)

In essence the sacrifice of all worldly or earthly things proves to
God our commitment to his kingdom and its required righteousness.

Very few people, however, are required to sacrifice all
earthly things. Most Melchizedek Priesthood holders will not be
asked to sacrifice in this manner, although some may be asked
to prove the depth of their commitment at some time in their life.
The Lord, however, is willing to accept the promise, the will,
and the commitment to sacrifice all earthly things even if the
deed is never demanded. In other words, we need to demon-

strate to the Lord that we would sacrifice if it were required of us. How can we prove this to the Lord? This attitude is crucial in knowing that our life is acceptable to God and thus obtaining faith to exercise the full powers of the priesthood.

The proof of our willingness lies in our ability to sacrifice what the Lord has asked of us. He has asked us to sacrifice ten percent of our income, to pay fast offerings, and contribute to the budget. Are we doing this? He has asked us to sacrifice the comforts of home to serve missions. Have we been willing to do this? He has asked us to keep his Sabbath day holy, to serve in Church callings, to home teach, to do temple work, and to serve in other ways. In short, are we keeping the commandments? The only way to truly show God our willingness to sacrifice all is by sacrificing what is asked. In this manner our faith grows, and we can know that our life is pleasing to God, that he accepts us and will give us the Holy Ghost to enable us to know his will in the exercise of all our responsibilities. There is no other basis upon which a true foundation can be built.

Before leaving this topic it would be well to remember that no man except Jesus has been perfectly pleasing to God in every way. God does not require absolute perfection in his sons before they can administer the blessings of the priesthood. If he did, these blessings would never be administered. But God does require a deep commitment, a hunger and thirst for righteousness, and a constant effort at improvement. This is implied in the phrase "endure to the end." The Lord desires constant growth, not stagnation. Endurance comes with pressing "forward with steadfastness" (2 Nephi 31:20). Faith grows in accordance with that improvement. God, like every father, is pleased with every faltering step his children take forward, but he will not be satisfied with anything less than a true king of righteousness, a prince of peace, patterned after the example of his Son. These principles are also true for all his daughters who would become "elect" ladies. We are promised that if we strive with all our souls to fulfill his commandments, making his will our own, "his grace is sufficient" and will take care of our weaknesses and deficiencies:

Yea, come unto Christ, and be perfected in him, and deny yourselves of all ungodliness; and if ye shall deny yourselves of all ungodliness, and love God with all your might, mind and strength, then is his grace sufficient for you, that by his grace ye may be perfect in Christ; and if by the grace of God ye are perfect in Christ, ye can in nowise deny the power of God (Moroni 10:32).

A Oneness with the Godhead

It is appropriate here to mention the promise God makes to the faithful priesthood bearer concerning the eternities. We have already seen that a "continuation of the seeds," or eternal increase, results from magnifying the priesthood through keeping priesthood and temple covenants. In the previous pages the scriptures have shown that the priesthood must be exercised in accordance with God's will. This implies a oneness with God. A righteous life promotes this oneness and gives confidence that an individual's life is accepted by God. Having proved on earth the ability to be one with God through the righteous magnification of priesthood callings, one has the promise of a total oneness with the Father through the eternities. This is plainly stated in the oath and covenant of the priesthood:

> And also all they who receive this priesthood receive me, saith the Lord;
> For he that receiveth my servants receiveth me;
> And he that receiveth me receiveth my Father;
> *And he that receiveth my Father receiveth my Father's kingdom; therefore all that my Father hath shall be given unto him.*
> And this is according to the oath and covenant which belongeth to the priesthood. (D&C 84:35–39, italics added.)

The ultimate goal of true kings of righteousness is this oneness with the Father. When they have made God's will their own, the Father can without hesitation give his proven sons "all that [he] hath." In a sense they have proven they can think, act, feel, and serve like God and therefore can be entrusted with his kingdom.

And he gave some, apostles; and some, prophets; and some, evangelists; and some, pastors and teachers; for the perfecting of the saints, for the work of the ministry, for the edifying of the body of Christ: till we all come in the unity of the faith, and of the knowledge of the Son of God, unto a perfect man, unto the measure of the stature of the fulness of Christ: that we henceforth be no more children, tossed to and fro, and carried about with every wind of doctrine, by the sleight of men, and cunning craftiness, whereby they lie in wait to deceive.

—Ephesians 4:11–14

CHAPTER EIGHT

Receiving
His Servants

The previous chapter concluded with a quotation from the oath and covenant of the priesthood found in Doctrine and Covenants 84. This chapter will deal with one aspect of this oath that is critical to fully magnifying one's calling in the priesthood. It is often spoken of, but usually in another context. Emphasizing it as part of the oath and covenant of the priesthood gives it fuller application.

The oath reads in part, "And also all they who receive this priesthood receive me, saith the Lord; for he that *receiveth my servants* receiveth me" (D&C 84:35–36, italics added).

This is an injunction to all the world to "receive" the servants of the Lord who hold the priesthood, for they come in his name. This is true of all who hold the Melchizedek Priesthood in righteousness, be they missionaries, bishops, or home teachers. However, it is also an exhortation to holders of the priesthood to "receive" the Lord's specially appointed servants who serve in the capacity of leadership, namely, the General Authorities and the local authorities. Priesthood holders should set the example in following the Brethren, for they are the Lord's servants in a very special way. The prophet and the Apostles are the Lord's servants. Local leaders—stake presidents, bishops, quorum leaders, and others—are also servants of the Lord. Their calls fall under this category, for all these callings are priesthood related. An individual priesthood holder cannot fulfill the oath and covenant of the priesthood unless he "receives" the men who hold these positions. But just how should we receive the leadership of the Church?

We will concentrate in this chapter on the correct attitude a king of righteousness must cultivate in order to receive the prophets and Apostles. This is not to rule out other priesthood offices. Indeed, every Melchizedek Priesthood bearer should apply these principles as they relate to all positions of authority in the Church; but by focusing our discussion in this way, we will be able to more accurately and completely define the essential principles as drawn from the scriptures.

Live by Every Word of God

How does one receive a prophet or an Apostle? The Lord gives a good guideline. He exhorts us to "beware concerning yourselves, to give diligent heed to the words of eternal life. For you shall live by every word that proceedeth forth from the mouth of God. For the word of the Lord is truth, and whatsoever is truth is light, and whatsoever is light is Spirit, even the Spirit of Jesus Christ." (D&C 84:43-45.)

The words of eternal life that proceed from the mouth of God most commonly come through his Apostles and prophets. Giving diligent heed to those words is the most important way of receiving God's servants. This implies not only listening to them but also following their counsel. Far too often, however, the reaction of some Church members, including those who hold the Melchizedek Priesthood, is that described so powerfully by the prophet Ezekiel:

Also, thou son of man, the children of thy people still are talking against thee by the walls and in the doors of the houses, and speak one to another, every one to his brother, saying, Come, I pray you, and hear what is the word that cometh forth from the Lord.

And they come unto thee as the people cometh, and they sit before thee as my people, and they hear thy words, but they will not do them: for with their mouth they shew much love, but their heart goeth after their covetousness.

And, lo, thou art unto them as a very lovely song of one that hath a pleasant voice, and can play well on an instrument: for they hear thy words, but they do them not.

And when this cometh to pass, (lo, it will come,) then shall they know that a prophet hath been among them. (Ezekiel 33:30–33.)

To emphasize the need to obey the counsels of prophets, the Lord prefaced the Doctrine and Covenants with the following words: "For verily the voice of the Lord is unto all men, and there is none to escape. . . . And the voice of warning shall be unto all people, by the mouths of my disciples, whom I have chosen in these last days. . . . Behold, this is mine authority, and the authority of my servants." (D&C 1:2, 4, 6.) This preface concludes with the phrase, "What I the Lord have spoken, I have spoken . . . ; whether by mine own voice or by the voice of my servants, it is the same" (D&C 1:38).

These statements are plain and irrefutable. Although many excuses may be given for failure to heed the words of God's prophets and Apostles, obedience is nonetheless required. The Lord stresses that obedience emphatically in Doctrine and Covenants 68:

And, behold, and lo, this is an ensample unto all those who were ordained unto this priesthood, whose mission is appointed unto them to go forth—

And this is the ensample unto them, that they shall speak as they are moved upon by the Holy Ghost.

And whatsoever they shall speak when moved upon by the Holy Ghost shall be scripture, shall be the will of the Lord, shall be the mind of the Lord, shall be the word of the Lord, shall be the voice of the Lord, and the power of God unto salvation.

Behold, this is the promise of the Lord unto you, O ye my servants. (D&C 68:2–5.)

A Unified Testimony

In emphasizing these verses, let us realize that the Lord is not requiring blind obedience. We do not believe in blind obedience. The very idea is foreign to the doctrine of the priesthood and the Church. We believe in trust—a trust that is born when one recognizes the "intelligence" of the "noble and great ones" (Abraham 3:22–23) foreordained to priesthood callings in the premortal councils. Alma spoke of this in his great speech on the priesthood:

> And those priests were ordained after the order of his Son, in a manner that thereby the people might know in what manner to look forward to his Son for redemption.
> And this is the manner after which they were ordained —being called and prepared from the foundation of the world according to the foreknowledge of God, on account of their exceeding faith and good works; in the first place being left to choose good or evil; therefore they having chosen good, and exercising exceedingly great faith, are called with a holy calling, yea, with that holy calling which was prepared with, and according to, a preparatory redemption for such. (Alma 13:2–3.)

Aside from trust, the Lord requires that we sustain or receive his servants, based on a personal witness which comes from the Holy Ghost. This too negates the idea of blind obedience. This responsibility is delineated by the Lord in Doctrine and Covenants 50, where he explains that those who are "ordained of me . . . to preach the word of truth" must preach it "by the Comforter." If it is taught "by some other way it is not of God." (D&C 50:14–18.)

How does one know another is teaching truth by the Comforter? The scriptures are plain on this subject. As Melchizedek Priesthood holders and as members of the Church we have as much responsibility to receive the word of truth by the Comforter as the prophets have to teach by the Comforter: "And again, he that receiveth the word of truth, doth he receive it by the Spirit of truth or some other way? If it be some other way it is not of God." (D&C 50:19–20.)

The oath and covenant of the priesthood explains that men are to receive God's servants. In Doctrine and Covenants 50 the Lord gives light on how to properly receive. Each individual must receive by the Spirit. As if to emphasize the simplicity of God's method of giving and receiving light, truth and counsel, the next verses state: "Therefore, why is it that ye cannot understand and know, that he that receiveth the word by the Spirit of truth receiveth it as it is preached by the Spirit of truth? Wherefore, he that preacheth and he that receiveth, understand one another, and both are edified and rejoice together." (D&C 50:21-22.)

A unity that brings rejoicing and edification is implied here. This is the spirit of the priesthood. Ideally, then, when the prophet speaks (for instance, at a general conference), each Melchizedek Priesthood holder, and indeed all members, should listen by the Spirit and receive from the Holy Ghost a witness. Then we stand spiritually next to the prophet and not behind him, and we naturally obey his counsel. This obedience is to the Spirit as much as it is to the prophet. Priesthood holders everywhere can then present to the Church and the world a unified testimony. Instead of one man or twelve men speaking, thousands speak, bearing testimony to the will of the Lord.

The kings of righteousness should never present to the Church or the world a mixed signal through criticism, debate, doubt, ridicule, or hesitation. *The Lord will never give a mixed signal to the sons of Abraham.* He will never give a mixed signal to the general Church membership. If we disagree with the commandments and counsels of God as presented by the prophets and Apostles, our problem probably lies in our own inability to truly listen by the Holy Ghost, not in the prophets' and Apostles' inability to teach by the Spirit. The responsibility to accept God's servants is ours. When a man accepts that critical aspect of the oath and covenant of the priesthood and learns to listen with the Holy Ghost, he will rejoice together with priesthood authorities and heed their counsel. All must be careful not to be guilty of pointing accusatory fingers at the Lord's servants rather than receiving them.

Whenever a person holds a doctrine, idea, or criticism which goes against the unified will of the General Authorities and the major body of Melchizedek Priesthood holders worldwide, that person is on a sandy foundation. There is safety in that vast body of witnesses. David spoke of these ideas in this way: "Behold, how good and how pleasant it is for brethren to dwell together in unity!" (Psalm 133:1.)

His Hands Were Steady

There is a beautiful story told in the Old Testament that gives a perfect picture of priesthood unity. It is found in Exodus 17. A battle is going to be fought between the Israelites and the Amalekites.

> And Moses said unto Joshua, Choose us out men, and go out, fight with Amalek: to morrow I will stand on the top of the hill with the rod of God in mine hand.
>
> So Joshua did as Moses had said to him, and fought with Amalek: and Moses, Aaron, and Hur went up to the top of the hill.
>
> And it came to pass, when Moses held up his hand, that Israel prevailed: and when he let down his hand, Amalek prevailed.
>
> But Moses' hands were heavy; and they took a stone, and put it under him, and he sat thereon; and Aaron and Hur stayed up his hands, the one on the one side, and the other on the other side; and his hands were steady until the going down of the sun. (Exodus 17:9–12.)

These verses can be related to today. The covenant children of Israel today also fight battles. Our battles are against worldliness, Satan, and evil. They are spiritual battles. Our prophet stands on a spiritual hill holding the rod of God, or the word and authority of the Father and the Son. It is a heavy burden to bear, and his hands are often heavy. If he carries the word high, the people of the Church prevail in the battle. The modern prophet needs to be upheld and sustained as Moses was by Aaron and Hur.

The picture of Moses holding high the rod of the Lord being supported by two other men in order for the people to prevail is symbolic. The prophet today is sustained and supported by counselors, as are all other priesthood presidents. All priesthood holders should view themselves as Aaron and Hur, who support and sustain and uphold the prophet through their own testimonies and obedience; such action will allow the general Church membership to prevail. How foolish it would have been for Aaron and Hur to criticize Moses for the heaviness of his hands! That would have been like adding weights to his arms. Let all the priesthood follow their example.

Noble and Great Intelligences

We have discussed the duty of the sons of Abraham to sustain and receive God's servants and have attempted to understand how that should be accomplished in order to present a unified multiple witness of God's will to the Church and to the world. Let us now examine more closely the servants themselves and why we can have confidence in them and receive them, particularly the prophet and Apostles.

It is important to understand the relationship of intelligence, or light and truth, to the priesthood. This relationship will correlate perfectly with all we have studied up to this point. Let us therefore return to Abraham and the instruction and vision he received after his ordination.

Abraham chapter 3, which is roughly divided into two parts, is critical to our discussion. The first half speaks of the stars and their relationship to each other:

> And I saw the stars, that they were very great, and that one of them was nearest unto the throne of God; and there were many great ones which were near unto it;
>
> And the Lord said unto me: These are the governing ones; and the name of the great one is Kolob, because it is near unto me, for I am the Lord thy God: I have set this one to govern all those which belong to the same order as that upon which thou standest (Abraham 3:2–3).

As Abraham's visions continue, it becomes plain that there are greater and lesser stars and planets and that some stars ''are set to give light'' (Abraham 3:10) and order to the universe. In other

words, Abraham is shown a hierarchy, or order of ascending degrees, among the stars and planets. In this same vision God
compares Abraham's seed to the numerous stars of the heavens.
We discussed this aspect of the vision earlier, but it is well to
keep it in mind in the context of all of chapter 3.

In the second half of Abraham 3, Abraham is shown a vision
of spirits. He learns that a similar relationship to that of the stars
exists among the spirit children of our Father in Heaven because
of their varying intelligence. In this way the first half of the chapter becomes a metaphor for the second. We are invited to compare stars with spirits. The following excerpt is rather long, but
is necessary for total understanding:

> And the Lord said unto me: These two facts do exist,
> that there are two spirits, one being more intelligent than
> the other; there shall be another more intelligent than
> they; I am the Lord thy God, *I am more intelligent than
> they all.*
>
> I dwell in the midst of them all; I now, therefore, have
> come down unto thee to declare unto thee the works
> which my hands have made, wherein *my wisdom excel-
> leth them all*, for I rule in the heavens above, and in the
> earth beneath, in all wisdom and prudence, over all the in-
> telligences thine eyes have seen from the beginning; I came
> down in the beginning in the midst of all the intelligences
> thou hast seen.
>
> Now the Lord had shown unto me, Abraham, *the intel-
> ligences that were organized before the world was; and
> among all these there were many of the noble and great
> ones;*
>
> And God saw these souls that they were good, and he
> stood in the midst of them, and he said: *These I will make
> my rulers;* for he stood among those that were spirits, and
> he saw that they were good; and he said unto me: Abra-
> ham, thou art one of them; *thou wast chosen before thou
> wast born.*
>
> And there stood one among them that was like unto
> God, and he said unto those who were with him: We will
> go down, for there is space there, and we will take of

these materials, and we will make an earth whereon these may dwell;

And we will prove them herewith, to see if they will do all things whatsoever the Lord their God shall command them. (Abraham 3:19, 21–25, italics added.)

We learn a number of things from these verses.

First, God is more intelligent than man. His wisdom "excelleth them all."

Second, Christ is "like unto God." He corresponds to Kolob, which was "nearest unto the throne of God."

Third, there are different degrees of intelligence among the Father's children just as there are different degrees among the stars.

Fourth, noble and great intelligences were designated by God to be "rulers" on the earth. These rulers were to give light, truth, and order to the lesser intelligences as the governing stars gave light and order to the lesser stars. (In using the phrase "lesser intelligences," I do not wish to give a negative impression. It refers to those children of our Father in Heaven who have not progressed in light and truth to the same degree as the noble and great ones. It also implies an order to the kingdom of God. These intelligences can become, with obedience and righteousness, noble and great also.) The noble and great ones were to receive light and intelligence from Christ because he was "like unto God," as the great stars received light from Kolob (see the explanation of figure 5, facsimile no. 2, in the Pearl of Great Price).

Fifth, the purpose of the earth's existence is to see if the intelligences can "prove" themselves by obedience to God. To do this all intelligences must recognize governing intelligence – certainly that of God and Christ, but also that of the noble and great ones, the servants of the Lord foreordained to be "rulers" on earth.

This beautiful comparison reaches the very core of the priesthood. As the stars and the sun give light and order to this earth, so the great Melchizedek Priesthood holders give light and order to mankind. Without the light of the sun, all life on earth would perish. Without the light of the Son and his gospel, man's spiritual life withers and dwindles into darkness. Without the sun's gravitational pull, the earth would spin its way on an endless journey through space. Without the governing control of prophets, Apostles, and other priesthood authorities, mankind recklessly spins out of control, ending in darkness and destruction. At the center of this whole system stands the Savior, he who gives light and control to his servants so that they in turn can give light and control to the rest of God's children.

These truths are powerful. Every true king of righteousness should allow the prophets and Apostles to give him light and to govern his direction. Thus he and his family may live spiritually. Likewise every true son of Abraham should recognize in himself, by virtue of his priesthood, the responsibility to be a "star" which gives light to and as appropriate governs in righteousness the posterity of God (particularly his own family), who look to the priesthood for guidance. This is done so that order, happiness, peace, and rest may exist among all God's children.

It is easy to see how this comparison ties in with all we have read about the priesthood. It corresponds with the family. It dovetails with the Abrahamic covenant and its responsibility of blessing all the families of the world. It stands side by side with receiving the Lord's servants, as the oath and covenant counsels. And with further study on the meaning of intelligence, we will see how perfectly it relates to Abraham's desires to be one who possessed great knowledge, to receive instructions, and to be a greater follower of righteousness. We spoke briefly of this in chapter 1. Let us now examine more fully the relationship between being a greater follower of righteousness and possessing greater knowledge, or intelligence and understanding, and being a king of righteousness, a prince of peace, a son of Abraham.

Intelligence

When we try to define "intelligence" as mentioned in the scriptures we immediately confront a number of other words and concepts. A familiar scripture states: "The glory of God is intelligence, or, in other words, light and truth. Light and truth forsake that evil one." (D&C 93:36–37.) Thus intelligence is equated with "light," "truth," and the "glory of God." Here we also learn that intelligence forsakes evil. Already we can see that intelligence is more than the accumulation of facts and degrees or the reading of the "right books." Learning and intelligence may not always mean the same thing. A deeper study of the Doctrine and Covenants reveals more synonyms that help explain the Lord's idea of intelligence. "For the word of the Lord is truth, and whatsoever is truth is light, and whatsoever is light is Spirit, even the Spirit of Jesus Christ" (D&C 84:45). Intelligence is associated with the Spirit, "even the Spirit of Jesus Christ." In section 88 the same relationships are taught: "My voice is Spirit; my Spirit is truth; truth abideth and hath no end; and if it be in you it shall abound" (D&C 88:66).

These added descriptions help in understanding what the Lord means by intelligence. It is more than learning. It is truth, light, and spirit. It is deeply associated with the Lord Jesus Christ.

Key to Receiving Intelligence

Scripturally, what are the key factors in receiving and maintaining intelligence in an individual? These are given in the same sections of the Doctrine and Covenants that define light, truth, and intelligence. Doctrine and Covenants 84:46 teaches that "the Spirit enlighteneth every man . . . that hearkeneth to the voice of the Spirit." In other words, one receives more light and truth as one obeys the light that has already been given.

Doctrine and Covenants 88 gives us a similar truth: "And if your eye be single to my glory, your whole bodies shall be filled with light, and there shall be no darkness in you; and that body which is filled with light comprehendeth all things" (D&C 88:67). Here we see that the direction of one's whole being, with all desires centering on God's "glory," will result in additional light and truth. An individual can be filled with "intelligence." Verse 68 continues with this line of reasoning and contains instruction on how to achieve a singleness of mind to the glory of God: "Therefore, sanctify yourselves that your minds become single to God." Thus we see that the sanctification of an individual results in the blessing of light and truth. We know from the testimony of the scriptures that that sanctifying process is contingent upon a person's acceptance of the atonement of Christ through repentance, baptism, and the reception of the Holy Ghost. The Holy Ghost then continues to purify and teach the person and thus help him or her to become Christlike.

Continuing in the Doctrine and Covenants we read, "He that keepeth his commandments receiveth truth and light, until he is glorified in truth and knoweth all things" (D&C 93:28). Obedience to the commandments is directly linked to receiving intelligence. That obedience becomes a sanctifying power which enables one to receive more and more intelligence. By contrast Doctrine and Covenants 93:39 teaches that intelligence can be lost "through disobedience." This teaching is repeated in section 1: "And he that repents not, from him shall be taken even the light which he has received" (D&C 1:33). It is also taught by the Prophet Joseph Smith: "As far as we degenerate from God, we descend to the devil and lose knowledge" (*Teachings of the Prophet Joseph Smith*, sel. Joseph Fielding Smith [Salt Lake City: Deseret Book Co., 1938], p. 217).

One more section of the Doctrine and Covenants follows that will solidify this point and allow us to make some conclusions before proceeding.

> And that which doth not edify is not of God, and is darkness.
>
> That which is of God is light; and he that receiveth light, and continueth in God, receiveth more light; and that light groweth brighter and brighter until the perfect day.
>
> And . . . I say it that you may know the truth, that you may chase darkness from among you. (D&C 50:23–25.)

The key to receiving more light is an individual's "continuing in God." Once again obedience is suggested. Alma teaches these same truths (see Alma 12). There is a consistency throughout all the scriptures.

A careful examination of these verses reveals the manner in which the noble and great ones obtained their degree of intelligence. They deserve to be "rulers" on the earth because of their righteousness and their "intelligence." Remember, Abraham desired to be a follower of righteousness and a possessor of knowledge and intelligence.

Full Confidence

The right to be a ruler with the priesthood is contingent on the degree of intelligence the priesthood holder possesses. Obviously the greater the intelligence, the more able a priesthood holder is to bless the lives of others. This is true of all members of the Church. Intelligence, we have seen, is acquired by righteousness and obedience. Possessing greater knowledge or intelligence comes as a direct result of being a follower of greater righteousness. Whenever we see a man who gives the world great depth and breadth of knowledge and truth, we can rest assured that he is a follower of righteousness. Joseph Smith is the great modern example.

Every Melchizedek Priesthood bearer who seeks to magnify his priesthood calling will desire to obtain more and more intelligence by following righteousness. This is the path a man follows and the blessings he receives when he tries to become a king of righteousness. In becoming a king of righteousness he also becomes a noble and great ruler of intelligence. This leads the man to a state when it will be said of him, "He is like unto God." With full confidence all can follow the great intelligences who stand as prophets and Apostles. All can have confidence in them, knowing of their righteousness and knowing that God has confidence in them.

No man can say he is fully honoring and magnifying his priesthood calling if he fails to fulfill the responsibility of "receiving" the Lord's servants. Failure to do so shows not only a lack of understanding of a basic element in the oath and covenant of the priesthood but also a lack of intelligence, for the most basic aspect of an intelligent man is his ability to recognize those with more intelligence than he. With this recognition he can be taught and can progress.

The elders which are among you I exhort, who am also an elder, and a witness of the sufferings of Christ, and also a partaker of the glory that shall be revealed: feed the flock of God which is among you, taking the oversight thereof, not by constraint, but willingly; not for filthy lucre, but of a ready mind; neither as being lords over God's heritage, but being ensamples to the flock. And when the chief Shepherd shall appear, ye shall receive a crown of glory that fadeth not away.

—1 Peter 5:1–4

CHAPTER NINE

Priestcraft or Priesthood?

In every dispensation of the earth's history the adversary has established his own kingdom to stand in opposition to that of the Savior. Not only does he set up his kingdom, he attempts to pattern it after the truths of Christ's kingdom. Satan is an imitator, mixing truth with lies and the scriptures with the philosophies of men. It should not, therefore, be surprising to find distorted parallels to the priesthood. Satan creates these to deceive mankind. Satan creates many different priesthoods to widen his authority. Let us concentrate on the most distinctive one—priestcraft. Understanding priestcraft will help us avoid the attitudes commonly found among the false priesthoods of Satan.

A Definition of Priestcraft

The Book of Mormon contains the best definition of priestcraft in the scriptural canon. After giving a detailed description of the characteristics of the Savior, Nephi warns against priestcraft: "He commandeth that there shall be no priestcrafts; for, behold, priestcrafts are that *men* preach and *set themselves up for a light unto the world,* that they may *get gain and praise of the world;* but they *seek not the welfare of Zion"* (2 Nephi 26:29, italics added).

Three basic characteristics dominate Satan's priestcrafts: (1) men set themselves up as a light; (2) men preach for gain and praise, or, as Nehor taught, "every priest and teacher ought to become popular" (Alma 1:3); (3) men do not seek the welfare of Zion.

All three of these are motivated by selfishness. The man or priest himself is the focus of attention or praise; he seeks his own welfare. All three of these characteristics are foreign to the motive underlying the true priesthood of God. As if to stress that true motive by contrast, Nephi immediately explains, "Behold, the Lord hath forbidden this thing; wherefore, the Lord God hath given a commandment that all men should have charity, which charity is love. And except they should have charity they were nothing." (2 Nephi 26:30.) By definition, charity "seeketh not her own" (1 Corinthians 13:5). Therefore, the basic motive behind all priesthood functions is charity, which reflects self-lessness. Let us look at what the scriptures teach about the true program of the Lord as opposed to the three satanic motives listed above.

Christ Is the Light

During his visit to the Nephites, Christ concluded his first day's teachings with the following commandment (notice how completely foreign it is to the first principle of priestcraft): "Therefore, hold up your light that it may shine unto the world. *Behold I am the light which ye shall hold up—that which ye have seen me do"* (3 Nephi 18:24, italics added). In the Savior's kingdom his ministers hold up his light, not their own. That light is reflected through following the example of the Savior—by doing and being all that he was and did. Christ also taught his Nephite disciples this truth when he asked them, "What manner of men ought ye to be? Verily I say unto you, even as I am." (3 Nephi 27:27.) True priesthood does not hold up its own light; the focus is entirely on the Savior, in both word and attitude.

Throughout scripture the Church is frequently compared to a candlestick or lamp stand. A candlestick does not produce light, but holds it up. This is a perfect analogy; the focus must be on the Savior, for he provides the light. Our own light in comparison to his is like comparing sparks to the sun, as Isaiah taught:

> Who is among you that feareth the LORD, that obeyeth the voice of his servant, that walketh in darkness, and hath no light? let him trust in the name of the LORD, and stay upon his God.
>
> Behold, all ye that kindle a fire, that compass yourselves about with sparks: walk in the light of your fire, and in the sparks that ye have kindled. This shall ye have of mine hand; ye shall lie down in sorrow. (Isaiah 50:10–11.)

The Praise of Men

The second characteristic of priestcraft is preaching for money, praise, or popularity. The danger of this motive lies in its tendency to promote doctrinal or behavioral change to suit the moods, beliefs, or desires of the people. After baptizing in the waters of Mormon, Alma the Elder established a church among his followers and ordained priests. He "commanded them . . . [to] labor with their own hands for their support" (Mosiah 18:24). The record then gives us the true motive behind honorable priesthood service: "And the priests were not to depend upon the people for their support; but for their labor they were to receive the grace of God, that they might wax strong in the Spirit, having the knowledge of God" (Mosiah 18:26).

A true Melchizedek Priesthood holder will desire as a result of his work the companionship of the Holy Ghost and the knowledge it gives. He does not seek for his own aggrandizement; rather, strength in the Spirit enables him to better receive revelation in order to more effectively serve and teach. He focuses on edifying the general Church membership and those with whom he labors. Once again a selflessness is implied. Payment for dedicated priesthood service is not praise or monetary gain but increased spiritual power and knowledge. Thus, the priesthood bearer becomes a more efficient instrument in the hands of the Lord or a taller candlestick which holds the Savior's light a little higher.

The Welfare of Zion

The third arm of priestcraft stated by Nephi was, "They seek not the welfare of Zion." By contrast Nephi teaches that "the laborer in Zion shall labor for Zion." Remember that Melchizedek "sought for the city of Enoch," which was called Zion (JST, Genesis 14:34). Zion by definition represents a people who are "of one heart and one mind," who dwell in "righteousness." During Enoch's time it was also called "the City of Holiness." (Moses 7:18-19.) Every righteous Melchizedek Priesthood holder, every prophet, has earnestly sought to create Zion, because only in a Zion society can mankind find a fullness of happiness, peace, and rest. This righteous desire was spoken of in the Doctrine and Covenants.

> Wherefore, hearken ye together and let me show unto you even my wisdom—the wisdom of him whom ye say is the God of Enoch, and his brethren,
> Who were separated from the earth, and were received unto myself—a city reserved until a day of righteousness shall come—a day which was sought for by all holy men, and they found it not because of wickedness and abominations (D&C 45:11-12).

In the true priesthood of God all men seek to establish the unity and righteousness of Zion. This is accomplished by covenanting to make all we have available to the Lord: time, talents, and material goods to the building up of Zion, even if it requires a sacrifice. This is the spirit of the law of consecration as it is explained throughout the scriptures, particularly in the Doctrine and Covenants. This does not mean that the focus of the Melchizedek Priesthood is on the programs or outward ramifications of God's kingdom. God's kingdom is his people. Zion is composed of people. The focus will always be on the individual members. When they are developing in righteousness, the kingdom's outward needs and organizations will continue and progress.

The Example of John

All three contrasting attitudes to priestcraft are beautifully portrayed by John the Baptist. His attitude and commitment should be an example to all priesthood members. As the Savior began to preach, John's importance diminished. John sent more and more of his disciples to the Savior. Among those who left John's group to follow Christ, some would become Apostles, including John the Beloved and Andrew, Peter's brother. Some of the Baptist's followers came to him saying, "All men come to him," meaning Christ. There is a suggested concern among John's disciples about the growing influence of Christ. John's answer is a masterpiece of priesthood attitude:

John answered and said, A man can receive nothing, except it be given him from heaven.

Ye yourselves bear me witness, that I said, I am not the Christ, but that I am sent before him.

He that hath the bride is the bridegroom: but the friend of the bridegroom, which standeth and heareth him, rejoiceth greatly because of the bridegroom's voice: this my *joy therefore is fulfilled.*

He must increase, but I must decrease. (John 3:27–30, italics added.)

It is easy to see that John sought not popularity, praise, or money from his followers. He held up the light of Christ and rejoiced when men focused on the flame and not the candlestick. He was laboring for the kingdom of Christ on earth, not for himself, and therefore he was content when he "decreased" and Christ "increased."

Self-Examination Is Needed

It would be well for all would-be kings of righteousness to examine themselves and see what attitudes direct their labors. The seeds of priestcraft are easily sown by the adversary, even within the ranks of true priesthood bearers. As priesthood bearers, do we seek for position in the Church and find ourselves criticizing those who are chosen instead? Is the praise of those who hear us preach or teach more important than the message or those who receive it? Do we love the teaching, the preaching, and the leadership more than what we teach or those we teach? Do we earnestly seek to build up the kingdom of God on the earth? Do our own light, our opinions, and our interpretations supersede those of the Brethren or the scriptures? Do we want to discuss or teach new, sensational, or titillating things? These and other questions should constantly keep us striving for proper attitudes. These are delicate areas and can be applied to all members, whether they hold the priesthood or not.

A Personal Reflection

I will digress for a moment and share some personal feelings on this subject. The subject is close to me, for I teach religion as an occupation. At the conclusion of an assignment I had held for three years, I was sitting in a testimony meeting with those I had served. I was moving to another state, and this would be the last time I spent with these people. It was an emotional meeting, with many tears, expressions of gratitude, and praise. All this produced within me a certain pride, a feeling of popularity and importance. "I really have done a lot for these people," I thought. Then the Spirit seemed to settle over me and conduct an interview of sorts. These were the questions the Lord asked me. I have never forgotten them.

"Whose children are these that are bearing their testimonies and expressions of gratitude?"

"They are thy children, Father."

"Whose Church is this that provides opportunities for leadership and service?"

"It is thy Church, Father."

"From whose scriptures did you teach?"

"Thy scriptures."

"When there was a Spirit in your classroom, your counseling sessions, and your conversations, whose Spirit was it?"

"It was thy Spirit."

"Whatever gifts or special abilities you possess were given to you by whom?"

"They were given to me by thee."

"If any lives were touched or changed, whose influence really made the difference?"

"Thine influence, Father."

"Then who are these people truly indebted to—you or me?"

"To thee Father, totally and completely."

It was a very humbling interview. I do not wish to demean the role of our individual contributions to the Lord's kingdom and to each other, but we should maintain our humility and recognize that we are tools in the Master's hands. It is his hand that guides and directs the work. To him and the Father go all the glory and the praise.

A Tumult of Opinions

A final example may help us see clearly the difference between priesthood and priestcraft. Nowhere will we find a finer example of the difference than in the testimony of Joseph Smith concerning the First Vision. Let us highlight the attitudes and characteristics of the priests of Joseph's day:

> For, notwithstanding the great love which the converts to these different faiths expressed at the time of their conversion, and the great zeal manifested by the respective clergy, who were active in getting up and promoting this extraordinary scene of religious feeling, in order to have everybody converted, as they were pleased to call it, let them join what sect they pleased; yet when the converts begin to file off, some to one party and some to another, it was seen that the seemingly good feelings of both the priests and the converts were more pretended than real (Joseph Smith—History 1:6).

Remember, Nephi taught that sincere charity is the true attitude of the priesthood, not pretended zeal. Christ referred to these attitudes when he explained to Joseph that "those professors . . . draw near to me with their lips, but their hearts are far from me" (Joseph Smith—History 1:19). Contrast this pretended love and enthusiasm with the comment Joseph Smith made while he was a prisoner in Liberty Jail, unjustly condemned by the world: "There is a love from God that should be exercised toward those of our faith, who walk uprightly, which is peculiar to itself, but it is without prejudice; it also gives scope to the mind, which enables us to conduct ourselves with greater liberality towards all that are not of our faith, than what they exercise towards one another" (*History of the Church*, 3:304). What a beautiful expression of the charity that is consistent with a Zion priesthood!

If we look carefully at the Joseph Smith account of the First Vision we will discover the real source of contention behind the religious leaders and their converts. In doing so let us remember that the Savior taught the Nephites that contention, particularly religious contention, was not of God but of the devil (see 3 Nephi 11:28–30).

A scene of great confusion and bad feeling ensued—priest contending against priest, and convert against convert; so that all their good feelings one for another, if they ever had any, were entirely lost in a strife of words and a contest about *opinions.*

My mind at times was greatly excited, the cry and tumult were so great and incessant. The Presbyterians were most decided against the Baptists and Methodists, and used all the *powers of both reason and sophistry* to prove their errors, or, at least, to make the people think they were in error. On the other hand, the Baptists and Methodists in their turn were equally zealous in endeavoring to establish their own tenets and disprove all others.

In the midst of this *war of words and tumult of opinions,* I often said to myself: What is to be done? Who of all these parties are right; or, are they all wrong together? If any one of them be right, which is it, and how shall I know it? (Joseph Smith—History 1:6, 9–10, italics added.)

Let us emphasize in these verses the word *opinions*. When men teach their own opinions there will be confusion, strife, and anger. Ideally, we would not want an "opinion" about the things of God, for opinions, by their very nature, are taught by those who are in varying degrees of ignorance about the things of God. This is part of the meaning of Christ's words to Joseph, "They teach for doctrines the commandments of men, having a form of godliness, but they deny the power thereof" (Joseph Smith – History 1:19). The commandments of men will be represented through opinions.

Revelation from the source of all truth is the only sure pillar to which we should tie our faith. An opinion is practically worthless. Opinions must be supported by "all the powers of both reason and sophistry." Opinions must be "proved" or "disproved." What a contrast to the simple testimony of a fourteen-year-old boy who said: "I had actually seen a light, and in the midst of that light I saw two Personages, and they did in reality speak to me. . . . I knew it, and I knew that God knew it, and I could not deny it." (Joseph Smith – History 1:25.) When Joseph went home to his mother after this vision he could say without opinion, "I have learned for myself." This is the power of the Church of Jesus Christ. Every member can say, "I have learned for myself," because we do not "deny the power thereof."

How does this apply to the honorable priesthood bearer. First, it is the responsibility of a king of righteousness to say, as did Joseph, concerning the great truths of the Restoration, "I have learned for myself." As priesthood holders we need to have a firm testimony of the doctrines, not opinions concerning them. Second, within our classes and quorums, our conversations and writing, let us not "teach for doctrine" our own opinions. They lead to "a strife of words," and we will find we need to rely more and more on "all the powers of both reason and sophistry" to establish our own opinion "and disprove all others." Zion is characterized by a oneness of mind and heart, not by a "tumult of opinions." Remember that a Melchizedek Priesthood holder is a prince of peace, not a spreader of contention or dispute. Joseph found truth by calling upon his Father in Heaven, not by simply inquiring after religion with all the "powers of reason and sophistry." There is a vast difference,

the difference that maintains selfless priesthood or can cause it
to dwindle into self-seeking priestcraft.

A Proper and Affectionate Manner

One final attitude that is worthy of examination is implied in
Joseph's account. Once again it portrays in a simple, direct
manner the difference between priesthood and priestcraft.

Joseph shared his experience with one of the ministers of his
day and "was greatly surprised at his behavior." This was the
beginning of a tremendous persecution and condemnation directed toward Joseph. Speaking of the years that passed between the First Vision and the appearance of Moroni, Joseph
said:

> During the space of time which intervened between the
> time I had the vision and the year eighteen hundred and
> twenty-three—having been forbidden to join any of the
> religious sects of the day, and being of very tender years,
> and persecuted by those who ought to have been my
> friends and to have treated me kindly, and if they sup-
> posed me to be deluded to have endeavored in a proper
> and affectionate manner to have reclaimed me—I was left
> to all kinds of temptations (Joseph Smith—History 1:28).

The attitude of priestcraft is one of exclusion, condemnation,
and persecution. In seeking to reclaim that which is lost, the true
king of righteousness exhibits an attitude of charity, forgiveness, empathy, and a "proper and affectionate manner." This
was the manner of the Savior. Melchizedek, we have learned,
preached repentance to his wicked people and reclaimed them.
Priestcraft persecutes those who differ instead of endeavoring
"in a proper and affectionate manner to reclaim" the wayward.
Priesthood seeks and sacrifices for the lost sheep. Priestcraft
slaughters the lost sheep or drives them further into the wilderness.

Contrast again the attitude of the persecutors of Joseph
Smith or the persecutors of any people with that evidenced by
the Savior:

And again, how oft would I have gathered you as a hen gathereth her chickens under her wings, yea, O ye people of the house of Israel, who have fallen; yea, O ye people of the house of Israel, ye that dwell at Jerusalem, as ye that have fallen; yea, how oft would I have gathered you as a hen gathereth her chickens, and ye would not.

O ye house of Israel whom I have spared, how oft will I gather you as a hen gathereth her chickens under her wings, if ye will repent and return unto me with full purpose of heart. (3 Nephi 10:5-6.)

For this reason the Savior told the Nephite disciples to never cast anyone "out of your synagogues, or your places of worship, for unto such shall ye continue to minister; for ye know not but what they will return and repent, and come unto me with full purpose of heart, and I shall heal them; and ye shall be the means of bringing salvation unto them" (3 Nephi 18:32).

In our wards and stakes the men of the priesthood are to be careful to exhibit an attitude of true charity, empathy, and forgiveness to the less-active or struggling members of the flock. They should be careful not to cause contention by promoting their own opinions, doctrines, or interpretations. Pretended love, opinions, exclusion, condemnation, intolerance, or persecution belong to priestcraft and should never be manifested among the Savior's princes of peace.

And I, being fifteen years of age and being
somewhat of a sober mind, therefore I was
visited of the Lord, and tasted and knew of
the goodness of Jesus.

—Mormon 1:15

Let no man despise thy youth; but be thou an
example of the believers, in word, in conversation, in charity, in spirit, in faith, in purity.

—1 Timothy 4:12

CHAPTER TEN

Sons
of Aaron

One area remains to be discussed. It is a vital responsibility of
the Melchizedek Priesthood for it concerns the continuation of
the kingdom of God on earth. That responsibility is preparing
the young men of the Aaronic Priesthood. Joseph Smith taught
that the Aaronic Priesthood was "an appendage to the greater,
or the Melchizedek Priesthood, and has power in administering
outward ordinances" (D&C 107:14). Young men must be
trained in their own functions and be made ready to take on the
trust of the Melchizedek Priesthood. The major responsibility
for this teaching falls to fathers. Bishops and Aaronic Priesthood
advisors can contribute (and in those families where there is no
father or the father is less active they must provide the major
role model), but the most effective training comes from a
father's teachings and example. To illustrate this point I would
like to include an experience of a father with whom I am intimately acquainted. This experience is related with his permis-
sion.

In the Footsteps of Thy Father

"When I was a new father I was very concerned that I not fail my children. I knew that fatherhood was the most important teaching I would ever do. As my first child grew I experienced more and more anxiety. I did not want to make mistakes that would lead my children down the wrong paths or drive them away from their Father in Heaven. My anxieties became so pronounced that they occupied the major portion of my prayers. I asked again and again for the Lord to reveal to me what I needed to do to ensure the righteousness of my children.

"One Sunday during the sacrament the Lord touched my mind and gave me an answer. In my thoughts I seemed to be standing in the land of Bountiful at the time of the Savior's appearance to the Nephites. He had finished his teaching, and as I watched he called forth the little children to bless them as described in the seventeenth chapter of 3 Nephi. I stood about fifteen feet away from him. I was holding my own firstborn child in my arms.

"He took each little child, one by one, and blessed them. They were wonderful blessings of hope, righteousness, and dignity. I listened until I knew what I wanted for my own offspring. If I could put my children in the arms of the Savior, the blessing he would give them would ensure the righteous life I so desired. His blessing would relieve my own anxieties.

"I waited until each child had received the personal prayers of the Master and had departed with their parents. He was standing all alone at this moment, looking in the direction of the departing children. Then he turned and looked at me holding one last child who needed his touch. He studied us a moment. Then, as if he read my thoughts, he smiled and stretched out his arms to us. I approached him and laid my own tiny baby in his hands. For a moment I was forgotten as he communed, through love, with the tiny life he held. When he was finished he raised his head and looked directly in my eyes. The smile was gone and in its place was a look of gentle urgency. Then he blessed my child with these words: 'I bless you that you will walk in the footsteps of your father and become as he is.'

"His words entered deep into my heart and mind. I received their meaning and watched his smile return as he placed my sleeping baby in my waiting arms. In a manner that is consistent with the Master Teacher, both my baby and I were blessed. I knew that I could not relinquish my responsibility as a father. I had to guide my footsteps so that my children could walk in them with honor.''

I cannot think of a better way to explain what each father must do for his own children, nor what each son of Abraham must do for the sons of Aaron. As Christ's footsteps can be followed with perfect confidence, so must each Melchizedek Priesthood bearer walk so that young men can follow with perfect confidence. The boys of the Aaronic Priesthood would benefit greatly by knowing a true king of righteousness by example; then they too can become one. The priesthood father should not relinquish this responsibility to the Church, to its advisors or leaders, or to his wife.

There will be young men in virtually every ward and branch in the Church whose fathers for one reason or another will not or cannot teach their sons. I grew up in a home without a father and therefore have a deep sympathy for these young men. I am grateful for the positive examples of my priesthood leaders, an uncle, and my grandfather, all of whom taught me by word and deed the sacred trust of the priesthood. Those young men who find themselves in a similar situation need not feel discouraged. Our Father in Heaven will provide a way for every young man who desires it to learn the honors and responsibilities of the priesthood from worthy Melchizedek Priesthood holders. I found innumerable examples in the pages of the scriptures, which my mother taught me to search early in life.

A father must also teach his sons to understand and magnify their priesthood callings. Sons need to be taught the sacredness of the sacrament, knowing that the Savior himself blessed and passed the sacrament. They need to understand, in light of the Abrahamic covenant, the importance of home teaching and missionary work. They need to understand the significance of the outward ordinances. They also need to understand the oath and covenant they make with the Father.

Invite All to Come unto Christ

Rather than write at length concerning these and other duties which are dealt with in many other books, I will concentrate on one critical area detailed at length in Doctrine and Covenants 20. Deacons, teachers, and priests are all encouraged to "preach, teach, expound, exhort, . . . to watch over the church always, and be with and strengthen them . . . and also see that all the members do their duty . . . ; to warn . . . and *invite all to come unto Christ*" (D&C 20:46–59, italics added).

These duties comprise the instructions given to the Aaronic Priesthood in April 1830 when the Church was organized. The most important phrase of those instructions, which summarizes all the duties of the Aaronic Priesthood, is the command to "invite all to come unto Christ." This is also the essence of the Melchizedek Priesthood. Young men need to know of this responsibility and how to fulfill it. If their years in the Aaronic Priesthood are spent inviting all to come to Christ, when they receive the Melchizedek Priesthood and are called on a mission they will respond enthusiastically, and they will be prepared. They will have a foundation on which to build as they learn to magnify future Melchizedek Priesthood callings. The invitation to come to Christ is perhaps the main reason why the Aaronic Priesthood boy preaches, teaches, expounds, exhorts, and strengthens.

Most boys approach these responsibilities with hesitation and confusion, if not complete ignorance. They need to be shown how a twelve- or fourteen-year-old boy can invite someone to come to Christ. They need to understand the most critical method of strengthening the Church and seeing that the members do their duty. Some of these duties can be accomplished in Sunday School talks or home teaching lessons, but by far the most important method will be the boys' own examples.

No one should underestimate the righteous influence of a worthy young man. The scriptures are filled with stories about boys and teenagers who exerted a powerful example. For example, Nephi was "exceedingly young" but large in stature. The key to his life was his "great desires to know . . . God" (1 Nephi 2:16). The two thousand stripling warriors' faith and nobility was an example for the entire Nephite nation. Mormon was singled out at the age of ten to be the custodian of the plates; at fifteen his concern for his people and his testimony was so mature that he endeavored to preach to them and invite them to come to Christ. We could speak of Samuel, David, Joseph

Smith, and others. In almost all cases great men were great and righteous boys.

I hope a personal example will not be out of place here. A friend of mine shared the following with me:

"Shortly after my ordination to the office of deacon, I received a telephone call from my stake president. Stake conference was approaching in a few weeks and he wanted me to offer the opening prayer. I was terrified and worried about it up to the last moment. When conference arrived I remember sitting on the stand looking out over the congregation that stretched through the cultural hall and onto the stage. I arose after the opening hymn and offered the prayer. I don't remember what I said, only how good it felt to close my eyes so I would not need to see the many people. I never thought of that incident again until ten years later.

"I was home from my mission and spending the Christmas season with my family after a semester of school. A woman I did not recognize came up to me and said, 'I need to thank you.' Since I did not know who she was, I was quite surprised. I told her I was sorry but I didn't recognize her and couldn't remember ever doing anything for her that was worthy of gratitude.

" 'No,' she said, 'you would not know, but I must thank you just the same. When you were a twelve-year-old boy you gave the opening prayer in a stake conference. Do you remember that?'

" 'Yes,' I replied. 'I remember that very distinctly.'

" 'I was at that meeting. At that time in my life I was struggling. I did not have faith in my Father in Heaven. I did not believe he answered my prayers or ever heard them. I'm not sure why I came to the conference, but I sat down and listened to a twelve-year-old boy pray. There was nothing special in the words he used, only a confidence he had, a belief that someone was really listening to him. I thought, "If a twelve-year-old boy can truly believe there is a God who listens to prayers, so can a grown woman." That was all I needed, and since that day I have offered many prayers and I know that God hears them and responds. All these years I have wanted to thank that twelve-year-old boy.'

"I am sure you can imagine how I felt at hearing those words."

That twelve-year-old deacon didn't do anything special. He merely said a prayer, the most common occurrence in our church services. But that simple action became an invitation. I do not believe boys comprehend the power they hold to influence righteousness.

The Latter-day Stripling Warrior

In exhorting others to follow the Savior, young men of the Aaronic Priesthood need to understand one of the great keys implicit in obtaining the full powers of the priesthood and spoken of in the oath and covenant. That key is a trusting relationship with prophets, leading to obedience of their teachings. It is most dramatically portrayed in the story of the two thousand stripling warriors. The stripling warriors of Captain Moroni's time fought their battles against the armies of the Lamanites, but the stripling warriors of today must fight against the armies of Satan and the influences of the world. As recorded in the Book of Mormon, none of the two thousand stripling warriors died. Sadly, however, in the battle against the world, many modern warriors do die. They die spiritually, succumbing to the things of this world.

If we search the scriptures carefully, we can learn the key to the stripling warriors' preservation. That key is obedience to their prophet leader. If applied to the modern spiritual war that key will also help to preserve all the sons of Aaron. Helaman describes the stripling warriors in the following manner:

> But behold, it came to pass they had many sons, who had not entered into a covenant that they would not take their weapons of war to defend themselves against their enemies; therefore they did assemble themselves together at this time, as many as were able to take up arms, and they called themselves Nephites. . . .
>
> And now behold, as they never had hitherto been a disadvantage to the Nephites, they became now at this period of time also a great support; for they took their weapons of war, and they would that Helaman should be their leader.

And they were *all young men,* and they were exceedingly *valiant for courage,* and also for strength and activity; but behold, this was not all—*they were men who were true at all times* in whatsoever thing they were entrusted.

Yea, they were men of *truth and soberness,* for they had been taught to *keep the commandments of God* and to *walk uprightly* before him.

And now it came to pass that Helaman did march at the head of his two thousand stripling soldiers, to the support of the people in the borders of the land on the south by the west sea. (Alma 53:16, 19–22, italics added.)

There is power in the decision these young men made because they made it themselves. "They did assemble themselves together." Their decision did not arise from the prodding of their parents or the call to duty from Moroni or the exhortations of Helaman. It arose out of themselves. This is critical, but more critical is their choice of a leader. "They would that Helaman should be their leader." This point becomes more powerful when we realize that Helaman was the prophet at that time. Here then is our key. They chose a prophet to lead them and then "they did obey and observe to perform every word of command with exactness" (Alma 57:21). They lived their lives in such a way that their prophet leader spoke of them as his "sons" and stated "they are worthy to be called sons" (Alma 56:10). What a beautiful thought for a young man to live up to! Would it not make a difference in a boy's actions if his goal was to live in such a way as to be worthy for a prophet to call him son?

When the young men of the Aaronic Priesthood "assemble themselves together" and choose a prophet as their leader, following his commands with "exactness," they will be spared in their spiritual battles with the world and they will be "worthy to be called sons." But what do we find all too often with the young men of the Church? Sports heroes, movie stars, or rock singers become their "leaders," and they mimic their styles, values, and standards.

It is interesting in light of this to examine a desire of the stripling warriors' parents at the time of their conversion. The scriptures tell us the reason for the changing of their name from Lamanites to Anti-Nephi-Lehies: "And now it came to pass that the king and those who were converted were desirous that they might have a name, that thereby they might be *distinguished* from their brethren; therefore the king consulted with Aaron and many of their priests, concerning the name that they should take upon them, that they might be *distinguished*" (Alma 23:16, italics added). The key word here is *distinguished*. They wanted to be different from the world. This does not imply a separateness nor an aloofness; on the contrary, their concern for their fellowmen was great. Rather it exemplifies their desire to live a higher standard, to be distinguished through righteousness. In short, to be a "peculiar treasure" and "an holy nation" (Exodus 19:5-6). These are the words the Lord used to describe what he called "a kingdom of priests."

The young man who holds the Aaronic Priesthood should understand his Father in Heaven's call to come out of the world, be distinguished, and follow with exactness the counsels of the prophets and Apostles. All these issues we discussed earlier. All pertain to the Melchizedek Priesthood and magnifying its callings, and hence all pertain to the preparatory priesthood. All are critical if a young man is to invite others to come to Christ.

A distinguished life is well defined in the thirteenth article of faith. Aaronic Priesthood boys should seek to be distinguished in the manner described therein. They should judge all their activities, entertainment, literature, and other interests by this standard: "If there is anything virtuous, lovely, or of good report or praiseworthy, we seek after these things."

If the sons of Aaron are distinguished from the world through living the principles of the thirteenth article of faith, and if they follow the prophet, their lives will begin to reflect the light of the Savior—and that light will be an invitation to others to follow him. Truly magnifying his calling in the Aaronic Priesthood will make a young man Christlike, a fledgling prince of peace. Young men, therefore, need to pattern their developing manhood after the Savior's life.

During the teenage years that most young men in the Church hold the Aaronic Priesthood, they are seeking to understand what a "real man" is like. Often they follow the wrong role models. Of all the men who ever walked the earth, Christ is the greatest. He is the perfect example of a true man. He defines manhood. His character and attributes express manhood at its highest. What do we know of him? He was meek, gentle, kind, compassionate, thoughtful, obedient, self-sacrificing, empathetic, patient, and courageous. His treatment of women and children is especially exemplary. These traits are the traits of true manhood. They are also the traits described in Doctrine and Covenants 121 relative to the priesthood. Young boys, aspiring to manhood, need to know this or they will imitate the traits the world presents, including toughness, aggressiveness, sensuality, pride, egotism, and vulgarity. The "macho" image of the world is completely foreign to the Savior's example of manhood.

The world creates crutches to manhood: fast cars, stylish clothing, alcohol and drugs, loud music, athletic egotism, guns, money, worldly accomplishments. A true man will always measure his manhood by character, not by the speed of his automobile or the volume of his stereo. For a young man to honor his priesthood he needs to believe this principle. This will cause him to study carefully the life of the Savior so he can better understand how he should act. He will need to see his own father measure his manhood by a Christlike character and not the "toys" and crutches of the world which many men still need. Perhaps this is the most important responsibility of a true king of righteousness, for if he fails here, the future of his own posterity is in jeopardy.

The priesthood is a godly privilege. It takes a Christlike man to wield its influence. The sons of Aaron will invite all to come to Christ only when they themselves come to him and reflect through their own lives the light of his example. May they learn from their fathers and other priesthood leaders to be true men, not little boys pretending to be men with the crutches of the world.

Young men are the sons of God; Melchizedek Priesthood holders have been given the sacred trust of leading them to the fountain of all righteousness, where they will meet the Master. In the glory of his example the darkness of the world can fade away. Then they will be sons of God indeed.

Oliver Cowdery displayed a beautiful attitude as he described the restoration of the Aaronic Priesthood on the banks of the Susquehanna River. I believe every boy who receives the Aaronic Priesthood should be acquainted with it. Because of the Lord's desire that all worthy young men receive the priesthood, we as a people have perhaps developed too casual an attitude to its bestowal, partly because advancement comes with age, and each new ordination follows with the passing years. But as Oliver knelt and received the gift his attitude was one of deep reverence and gratitude. This is how he described that moment:

> But, dear brother, think, further think for a moment, what joy filled our hearts, and with what surprise we must have bowed, (for who would not have bowed the knee for such a blessing?) when we received under his hand the Holy Priesthood as he said, "Upon you my fellow-servants, in the name of Messiah, I confer this Priesthood and this authority, which shall remain upon earth, that the Sons of Levi may yet offer an offering unto the Lord in righteousness" (Joseph Smith—History, p. 59).

What a magnificent attitude is portrayed in the words "for who would not have bowed the knee for such a blessing"! I hope all young men feel this way and receive the "holy priesthood" with "joy [filling their] hearts." Then they will truly be prepared to bow the knee again to receive the Melchizedek Priesthood.

And again I say unto you, my friends, for
from henceforth I shall call you friends, it is
expedient that I give unto you this commandment, that ye become even as my friends in
days when I was with them, traveling to
preach the gospel in my power.

— D&C 84:77

CHAPTER ELEVEN

Friends or Servants?

At the Last Supper Christ addressed his disciples as his
"friends." He said, "Henceforth I call you not servants; for the
servant knoweth not what his lord doeth: but I have called you
friends; for all things that I have heard of my Father I have made
known unto you" (John 15:15). In the Doctrine and Covenants
the Lord also addressed Joseph Smith and the early elders of
the Church as friends. I believe the Savior offers to all the invitation of being a friend and to know "what his lord doeth."

There is a subtle difference between the servant and the
friend. The servant often serves without understanding. He,
perhaps, from time to time, will need to be reminded, prodded,
even compelled to do his duty. The friend shares the desires,
commitment, and goals of the Master. He serves out of love both
for his friend and for his fellowmen. He does not need to be reminded of his duty, but will be "anxiously engaged in a good
cause" (D&C 58:27). His dedication is born of deep respect and
compassion. This is a lofty goal to reach for, but I can think of no
higher compliment that could be paid than that of friend to the
Savior. May our service and commitment to the Lord's Kingdom

always aspire to be this basis. If it is, we will perform home teaching, fellowshipping, sharing the gospel, raising righteous families, and all other priesthood responsibilities in a manner worthy of the name Melchizedek—King of Righteousness.

I have tried in this book to portray the dignity of the priesthood. The principles we have discussed are lofty. God sets a high standard. No man, other than the Savior, has totally fulfilled the expectations of the priesthood. The greatest prophets of every dispensation have felt inadequate when confronted with the great responsibilities placed upon their shoulders, but they did not despair. With humility and trust in God they bore their challenges nobly and honestly. This is the way we learn, and God is patient with those who try. In many sections of the Doctrine and Covenants we read of the early elders' weaknesses and faults. We also read of God's continuing forgiveness and encouragement. "My grace is sufficient for all men that humble themselves before me" (Ether 12:27), the Lord promised Moroni when he was confronted with his own weaknesses in writing. His grace will always be sufficient, as long as we strive to live up to the honor of the priesthood.

Let all of us who share this honor not be discouraged, disheartened, or burdened with guilt because we do not always measure up in every way to the nobility of the priesthood. Rather, let us strive to walk the Lord's pathway steadfastly, "having a perfect brightness of hope" (2 Nephi 31:20). Let us also not compare our progress on that pathway with the progress of others, for this often leads to either pride or despair. As Paul said: "But let every man prove his own work, and then shall he have rejoicing in himself alone, and not in another. For every man shall bear his own burden." (Galatians 6:4–5.)

What is important to the Lord and to the Church is that we do progress along the path. Complacency or anxiety only hinder the climb. Remember that our Father in Heaven is pleased with every forward step, no matter how small. His gospel is one of rejoicing, gladness, and joy. It is dominated by hope. He desires his sons to become true kings of righteousness as was his Only Begotten Son. Until that day let all say, as Paul did,

Brethren, I count not myself to have apprehended: but this one thing I do, forgetting those things which are behind, and reaching forth unto those things which are before,

I press toward the mark for the prize of the high calling of God in Christ Jesus (Philippians 3:13–14).

Index